Mel Bay presents

101 Essenti
Rock 'n' Roll Chord
Progressions

Chord Diagrams Included • For All Musicians and Song Writers

by Larry McCabe

To Access the Online Audio Recording Go to:
www.melbay.com/99182BCDEB

ONLINE AUDIO

Track		Track		Track		Track	
1	"A" tuning note	26	Ex. 25	51	Ex. 50	76	Ex. 76
2	Ex. 1	27	Ex. 26	52	Ex. 51	77	Ex. 77
3	Ex. 2	28	Ex. 27	53	Ex. 52	78	Ex. 78
4	Ex. 3	29	Ex. 28	54	Ex. 53-54	79	Ex. 79
5	Ex. 4	30	Ex. 29	55	Ex. 55	80	Ex. 80
6	Ex. 5	31	Ex. 30	56	Ex. 56	81	Ex. 81
7	Ex. 6	32	Ex. 31	57	Ex. 57	82	Ex. 82
8	Ex. 7	33	Ex. 32	58	Ex. 58	83	Ex. 83
9	Ex. 8	34	Ex. 33	59	Ex. 59	84	Ex. 84
10	Ex. 9	35	Ex. 34	60	Ex. 60	85	Ex. 85
11	Ex. 10	36	Ex. 35	61	Ex. 61	86	Ex. 86
12	Ex. 11	37	Ex. 36	62	Ex. 62	87	Ex. 87-88
13	Ex. 12	38	Ex. 37	63	Ex. 63	88	Ex. 89-90
14	Ex. 13	39	Ex. 38	64	Ex. 64	89	Ex. 91
15	Ex. 14	40	Ex. 39	65	Ex. 65	90	Ex. 92
16	Ex. 15	41	Ex. 40	66	Ex. 66	91	Ex. 93
17	Ex. 16	42	Ex. 41	67	Ex. 67	92	Ex. 94
18	Ex. 17	43	Ex. 42	68	Ex. 68	93	Ex. 95
19	Ex. 18	44	Ex. 43	69	Ex. 69	94	Ex. 96
20	Ex. 19	45	Ex. 44	70	Ex. 70	95	Ex. 97
21	Ex. 20	46	Ex. 45	71	Ex. 71	96	Ex. 98
22	Ex. 21	47	Ex. 46	72	Ex. 72	97	Ex. 99
23	Ex. 22	48	Ex. 47	73	Ex. 73	98	Ex. 100
24	Ex. 23	49	Ex. 48	74	Ex. 74	99	Ex. 101
25	Ex. 24	50	Ex. 49	75	Ex. 75		

1 2 3 4 5 6 7 8 9 0

Visit us on the Web at www.melbay.com — E-mail us at email@melbay.com

Contents

Introduction

A few weeks ago a student from India brought a CD to his guitar lesson. According to him, the CD contained a traditional music soundtrack from a recently popular Indian movie. Listening to the recording, my ears were surprised to hear a pounding, synthesized disco beat playing throughout. Yes, there were also a few traditional Indian instruments playing along, and the singers were singing in a native dialect. But the Western commercial music influences were overpowering. To sum it up, it was a teaspoon of Ravi Shankar mixed with a quart of Michael Jackson.

It would have been difficult for the rock and roll pioneers of the 1950s to know that rock and roll, like Atlas, would someday hold the whole earth in its string-bending tentacles. From transistor radios to eight-track tapes to satellite dishes in outer space, we know now that rock and roll is not only here to stay, but that it is *everywhere* to stay.

The little transistors and the eight-track cartridges are gone now, but rock chord progressions have not changed much since the early days. With that in mind, I have compiled this collection of *101 Essential Rock 'n Roll Chord Progressions* for everyone who plays, writes, or works with rock music. The book contains all the important rock progressions you will ever need to create nifty rock songs, super stage shows, and awesome broadcasts for the entire global village. Enjoy!

Larry McCabe

Tallahassee, Florida

How To Use This Book

This book is for music students, teachers, performing artists, recording studios, composers, songwriters, advertising agencies, and any person or music company who desires a user-friendly, comprehensive guide to rock chord progressions. All creative musicians and writers who study, perform, or compose rock music will benefit from this book. In addition, the companion CD is ideal for jamming and ear training.

Each progression in the book is in the key of C major or its relative minor key, A minor. This format provides a consistent point of reference while facilitating ease in analyzing and comparing examples. If you wish to play some of the progressions in other keys but do not know how to transpose, you will find instructions for transposing on page 47.

A nice variety of popular rock rhythms is covered on pages 43-46. Each rhythm is easy to learn and can be played with many chord progressions.

The Chord Charts

Each chord progression contains the following information:

a) Chord names are supplied above each measure.

b) Chord frames (specific voicings) are supplied for guitarists.

c) Blank staves for both treble and bass clefs can serve as worksheets for study or composition.

d) Several types of progressions are covered, including 4-bar, 8-bar, and blues.

Other than the blues progressions, each example is unresolved in the book and on the recording. Although most of the examples can resolve to a C chord, they can move to other chords as well. Leaving the progressions unresolved encourages you to use your imagination when combining progressions.

Chord Symbols

Chord frames are included for guitar players. It is not important to use the specific voicings shown on the chord frames, although they are very useful for guitarists who are just beginning to learn chords. Keyboard players should have no trouble creating chord voicings from the chord symbols.

Creating Songs with the Chord Progressions

It's easy to combine short chord progressions to create complete songs. Here are a few simple examples:

1. Put two four-bar progressions back-to-back to create an 8-bar verse or chorus. You can use the same progression played twice if you wish. Or, use two different progressions for variety.

   EXAMPLE: Progression #3, played twice, becomes either an 8-bar verse, or an 8-bar chorus.

   EXAMPLE: Progression #8, followed by progression #3, becomes either an 8-bar verse or chorus.

2. Most of the 8-bar progressions can be used as a short verse or chorus.

3. Combine two compatible 8-bar progressions to create a 16-bar verse or chorus.

   EXAMPLE: Progression # 62, followed by progression #61, becomes either a 16-bar verse or chorus.

To learn more about song forms such as AAA, AB, AABA, etc. see Mel Bay's *You Can Teach Yourself® Song Writing* by Larry McCabe.

The Companion CD

1. An extended "A" tuning beep is provided on the first track of the companion CD.
2. The CD, recorded in stereo, is mixed as follows: The drums are in the center
   The rhythm guitar is on the right
   The bass is on the left
3. If you wish, you can remove either the guitar or the bass by turning down the appropriate speaker.
4. Because the current technology permits only 99 tracks, it was necessary to double a few examples on the CD.
5. The background is kept very simple to minimize clashing with your original ideas. If you would like to experiment with different rhythm patterns, see the *Famous Rock Rhythms* on pages 43-46.

Procedure

Because this book is not a graded method, you can work through the examples in any order.

Projects For Students, Musicians, & Writers

This book is designed to serve a wide range of individual needs. The following projects will benefit all musicians and writers. Teachers can assign the projects as needed.

1. Transpose each chord progression to several other keys.
2. Write out the *formula* (scale tones from which the chord is derived) for each chord in a progression. For example, the formula for a dominant chord (C7, F7, G7, etc.) is 1-3-5-♭7, meaning the first, third, fifth, and flatted seventh tones of the C scale.
3. Write out the spelling for each chord. The term *chord spelling* simply means the notes of the chord; for example, the spelling for C7 is C E G B♭.
4. Apply each formula (and transpose each spelling) to all root tones. If you need help with chord theory, formulas and spellings, see the tables in Mel Bay's *Blues Band Rhythm Guitar*.
5. Create several original songs by combining or modifying progressions from this book.
6. Keyboard players should write out logical voicings for the chord changes.
7. Try to learn several progressions by ear from the companion CD.
8. Instrumentalists: Jam or compose original solos, phrases, or bass lines to the chord progressions.
9. Songwriters and composers: Write original lyrics and music to the chord progressions.
10. Recording studios and arrangers can write or play "instant" original songs and arrangements to the chord progressions.
11. Advertising agencies can refer to the chord progressions for quick background ideas.

For further reference, see the following Mel Bay book/CD sets by Larry McCabe

- *You Can Teach Yourself Songwriting®* covers song form, chord theory, ideas for lyrics and titles, copyright, and other essential information and theory for songwriters and musicians.
- *101 Dynamite Rock Guitar Rhythm Patterns* teaches a great variety of rhythms for rock music.
- *101 Dynamite Rock Bass Patterns* teaches the famous bass patterns heard on thousands of recordings.
- *101 Essential Jazz Chord Progressions* teaches the hip chord changes used in jazz music.
- *101 Essential Country Chord Progressions* teaches the most common country chord changes.
- *101 Essential Blues Progressions* is a comprehensive manual of modern blues chord progressions.

A note to pros and teachers: The *101 Essential Progressions* books are indispensible for anyone who works with a variety of styles

4-Bar Chord Progressions

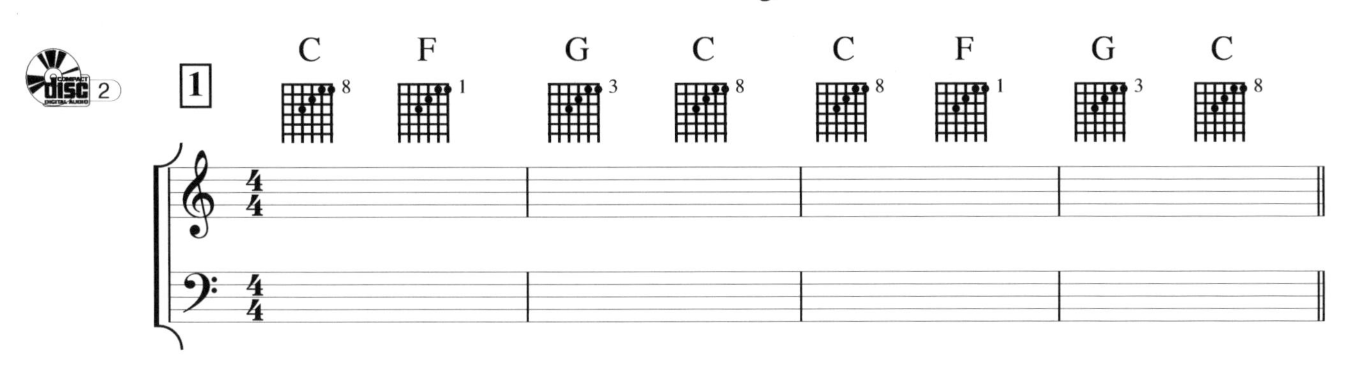

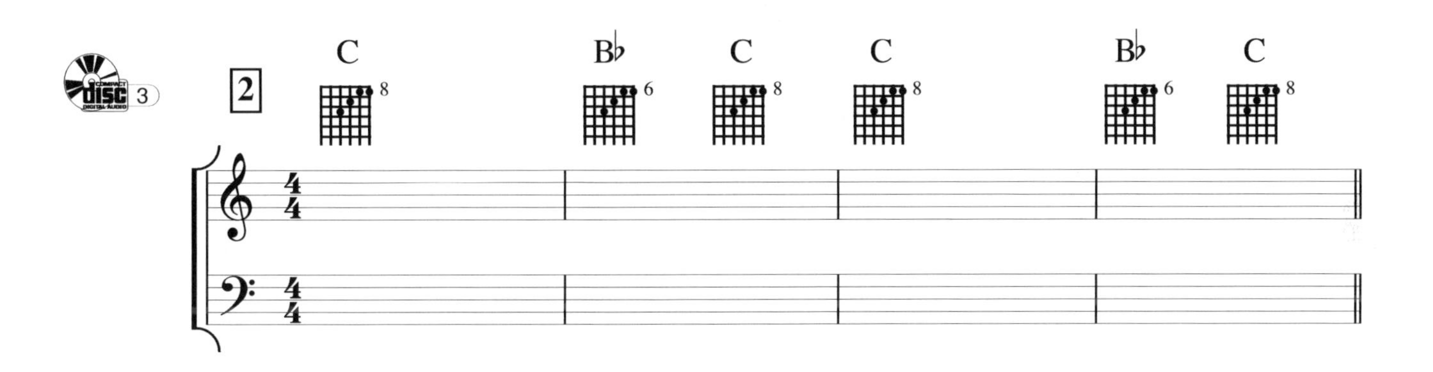

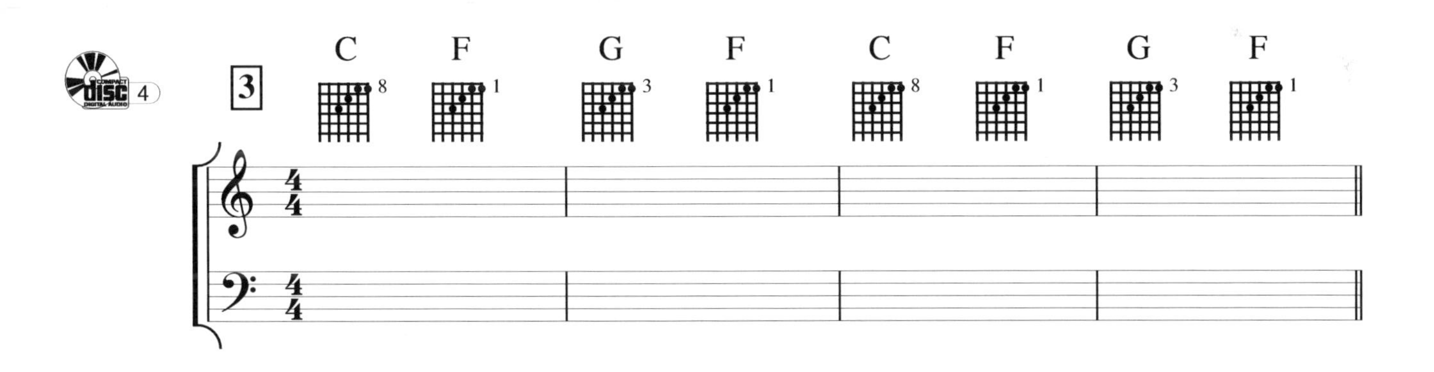

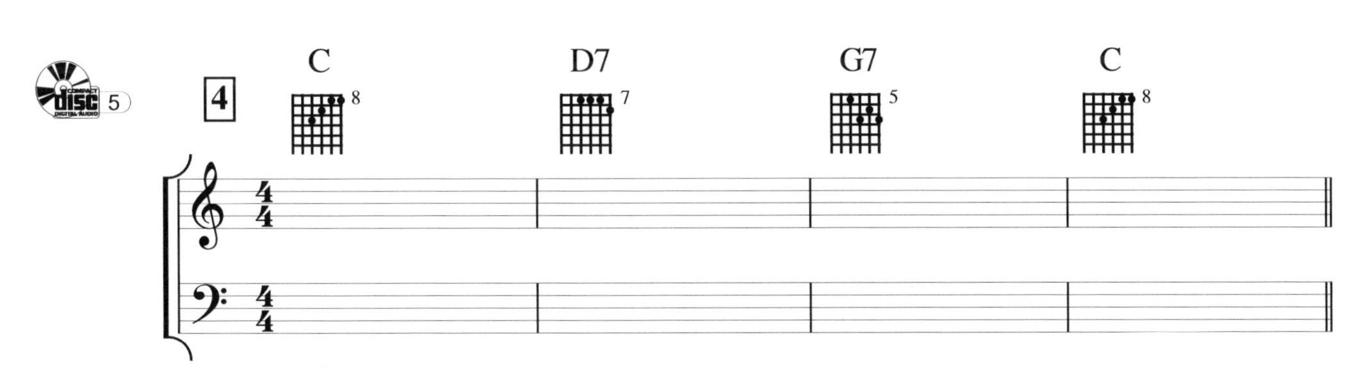

4-Bar Chord Progressions . . . continued

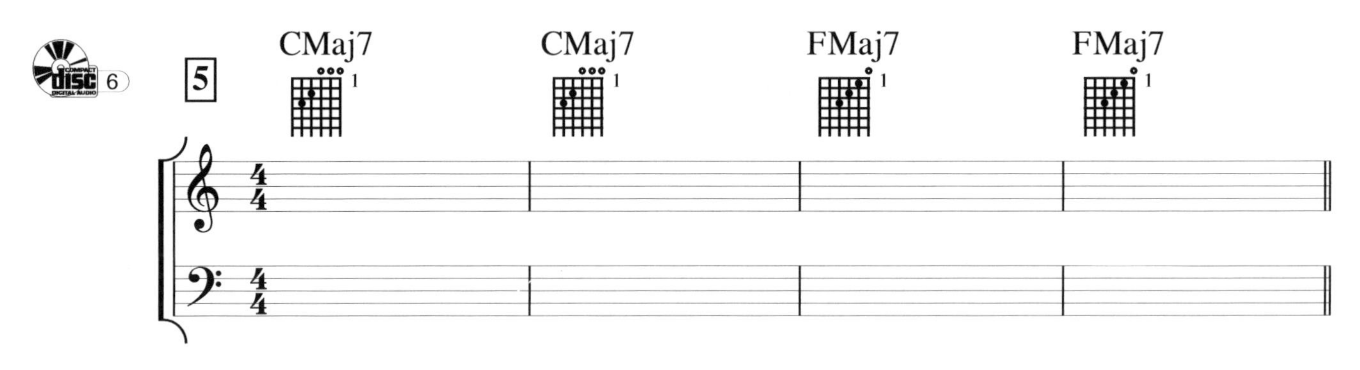

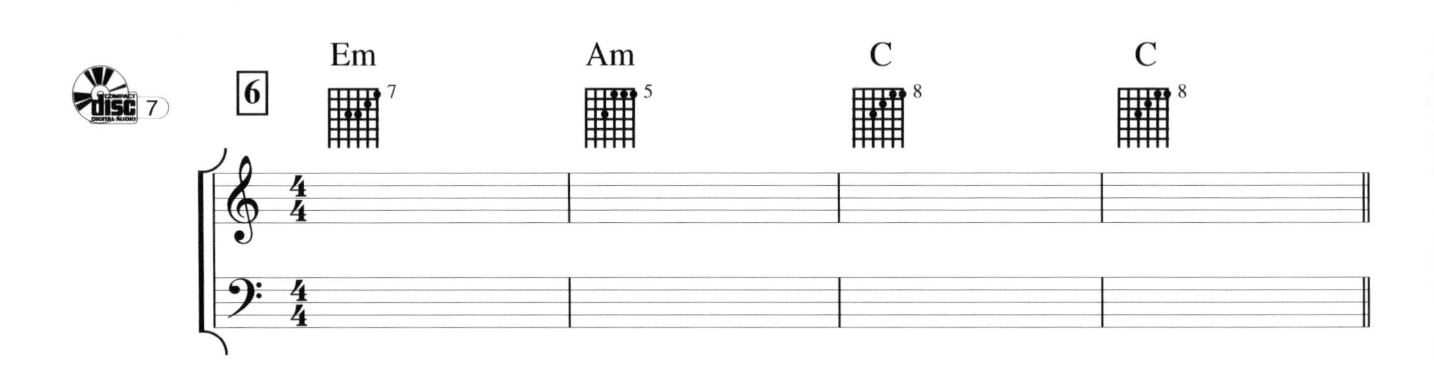

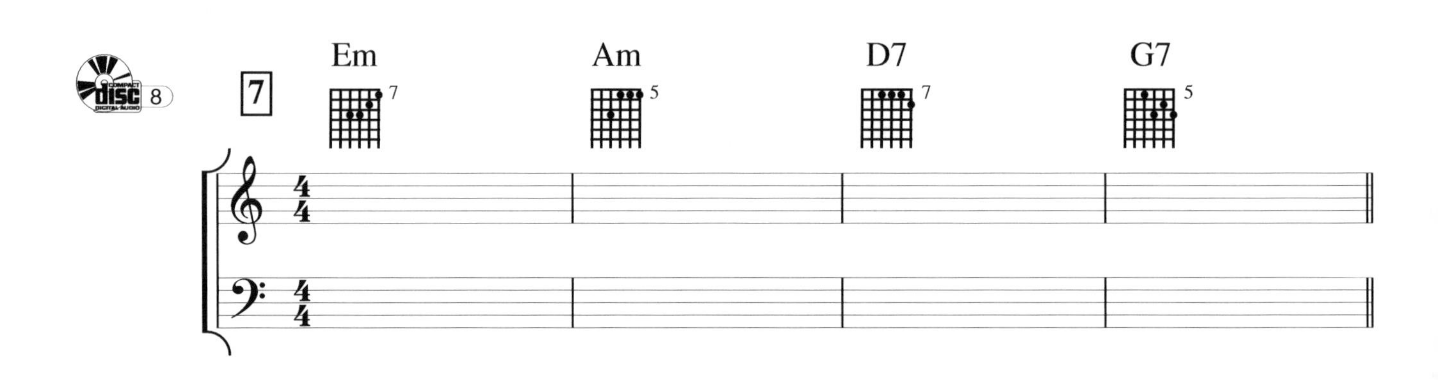

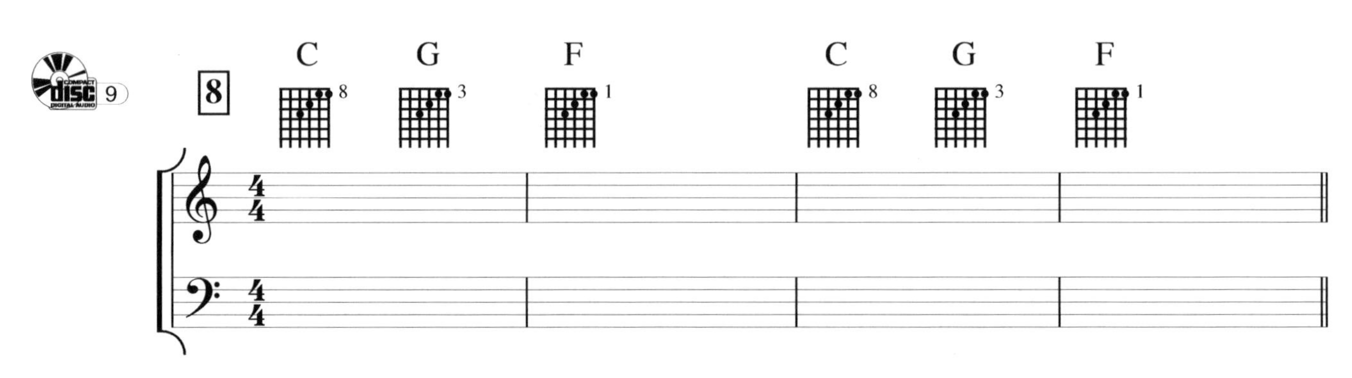

4-Bar Chord Progressions . . . continued

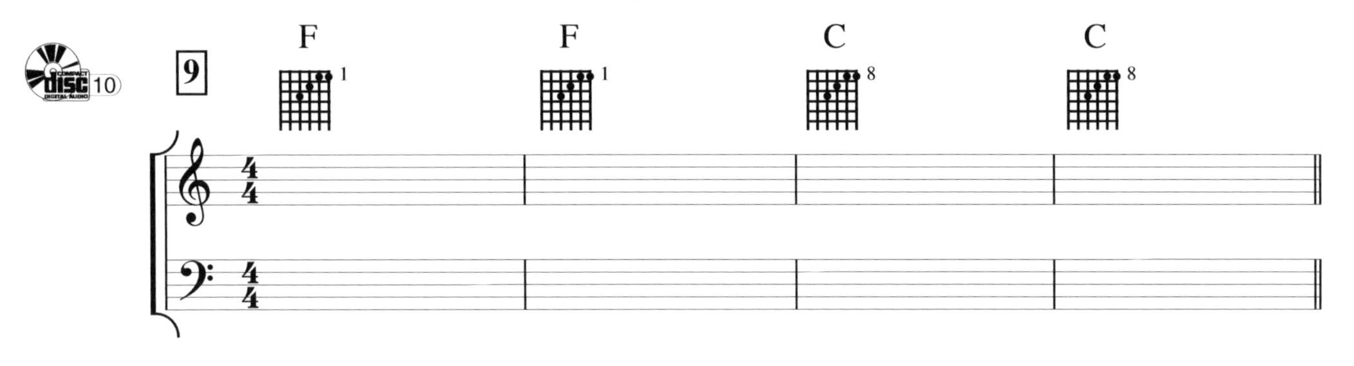

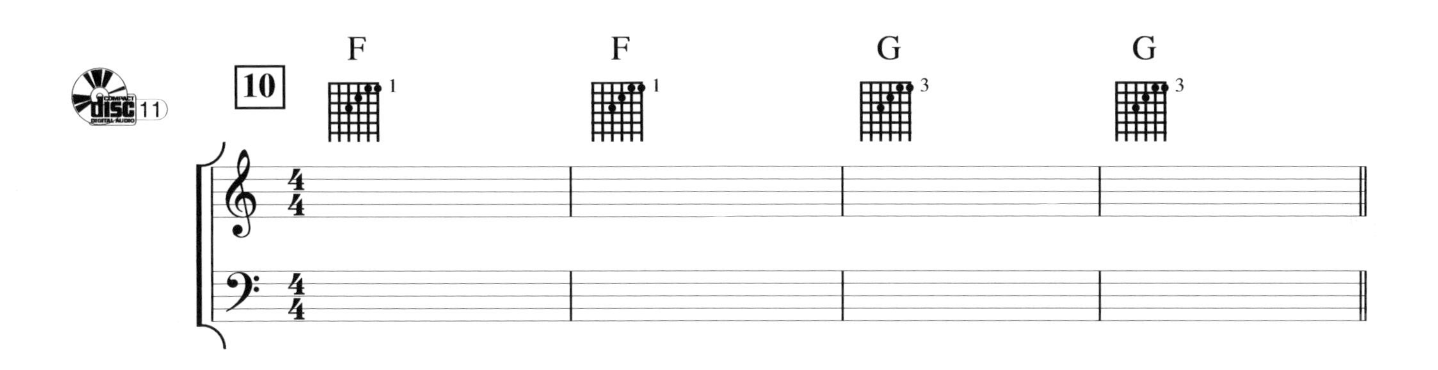

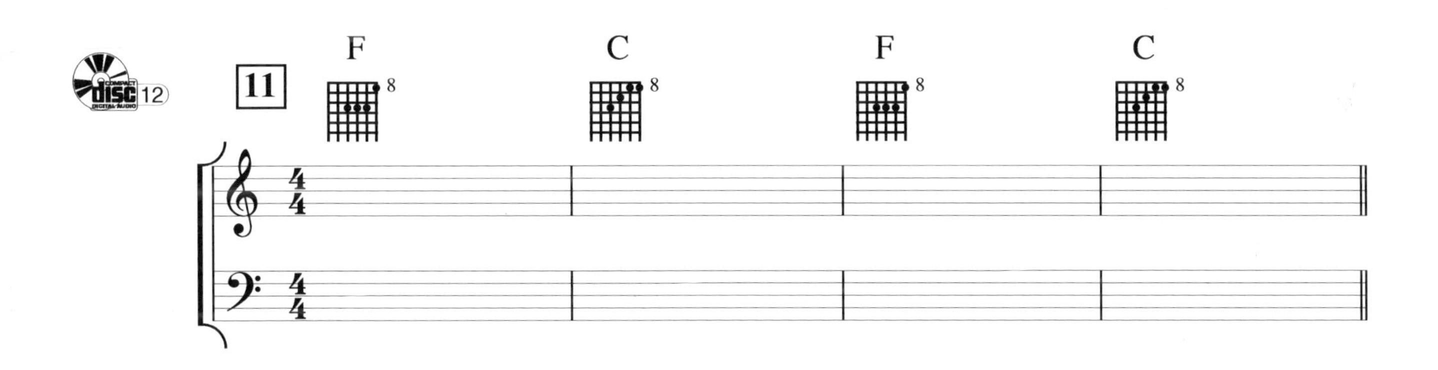

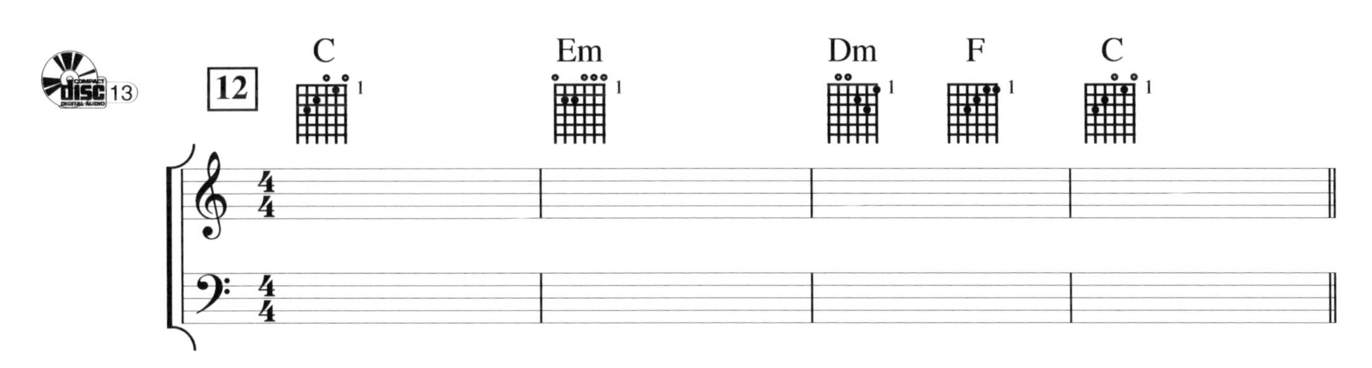

4-Bar Chord Progressions . . . continued

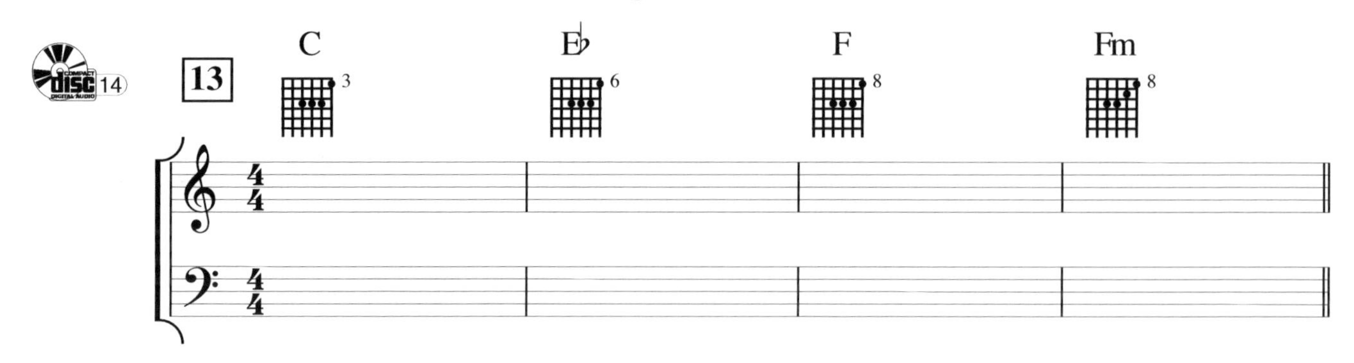

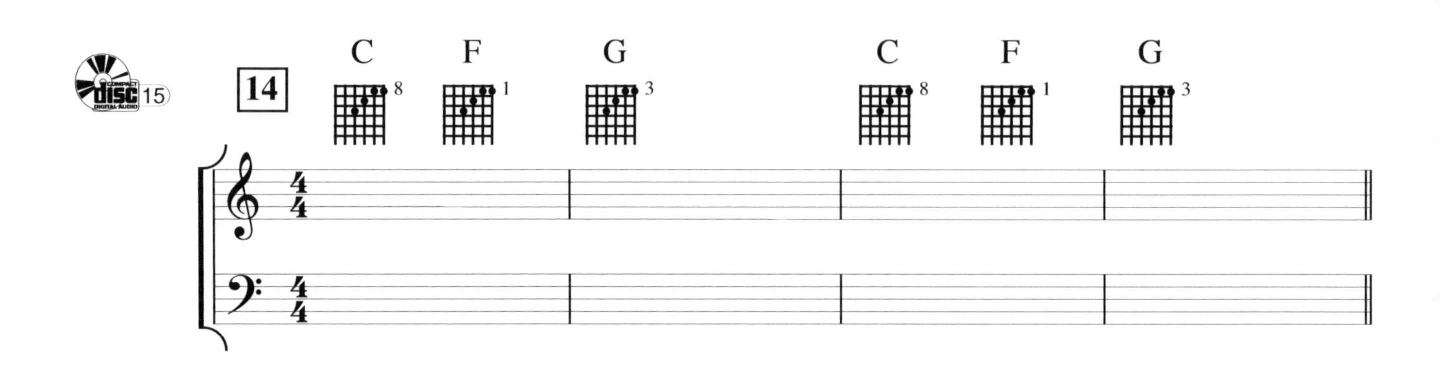

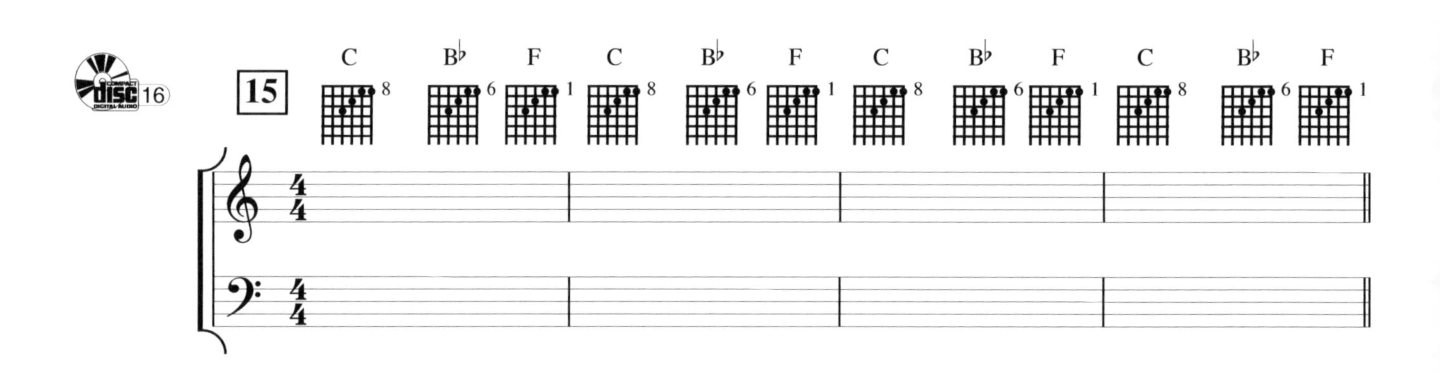

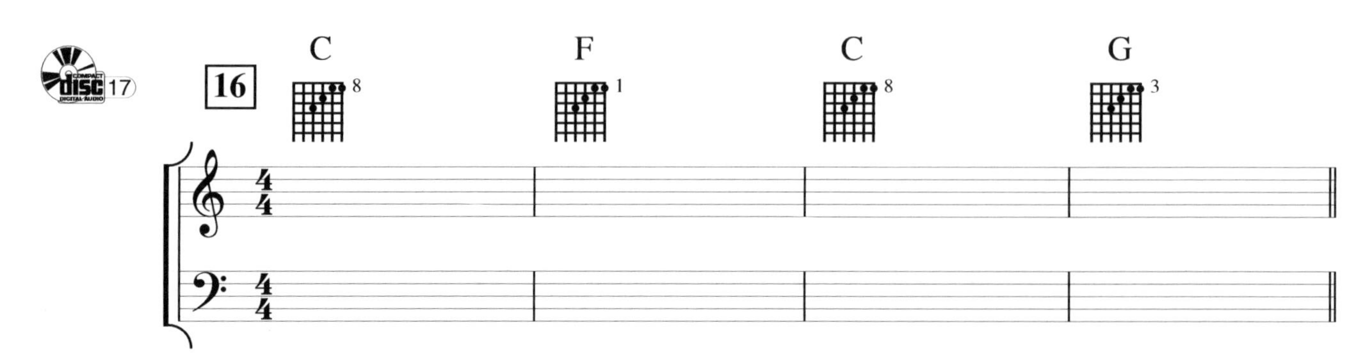

4-Bar Chord Progressions . . . continued

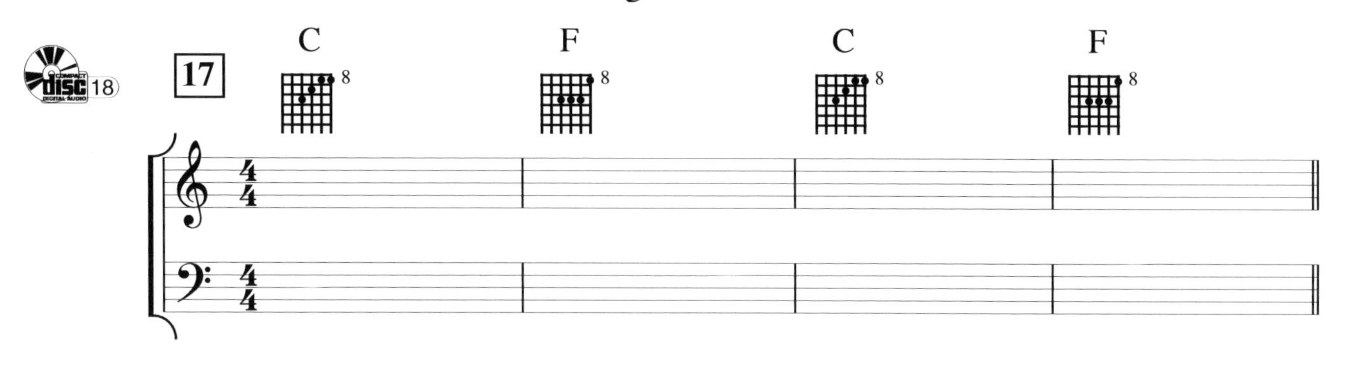

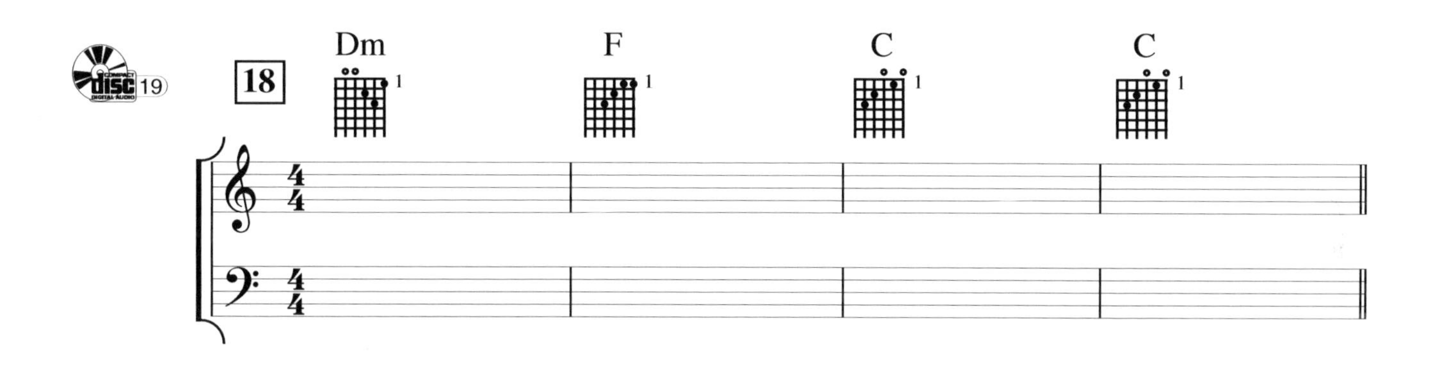

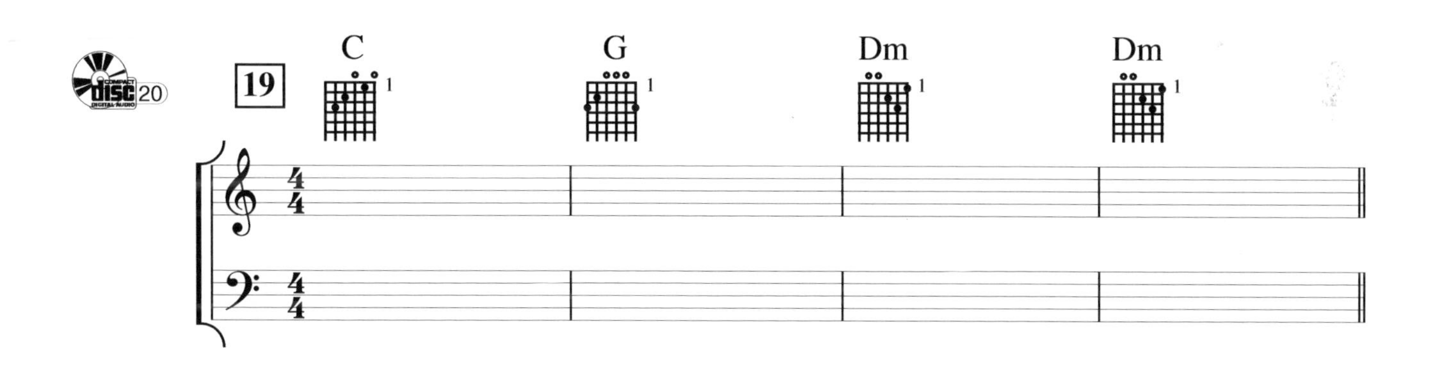

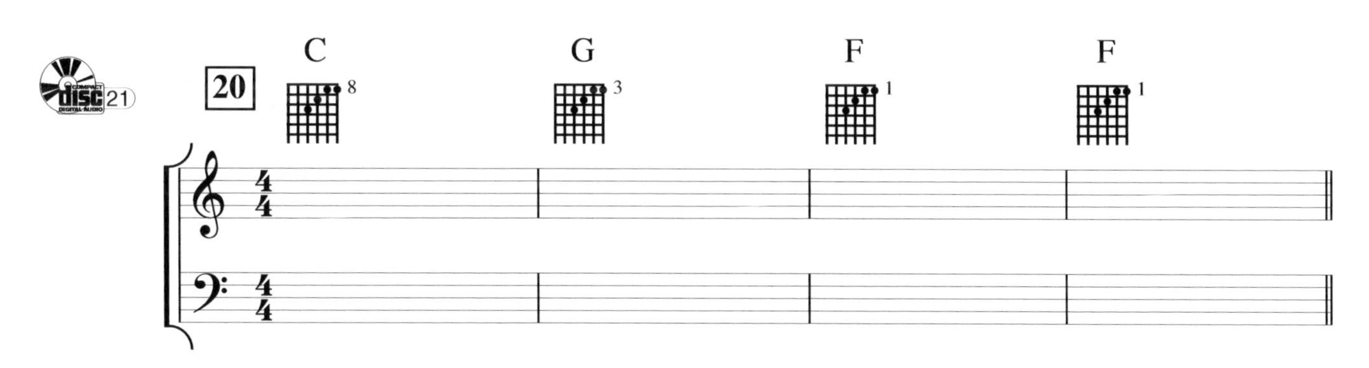

4-Bar Chord Progressions . . . continued

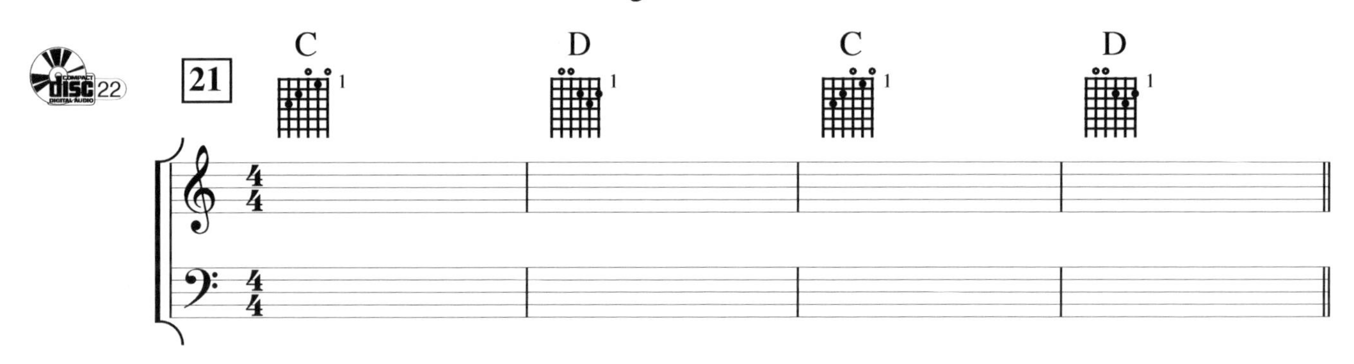

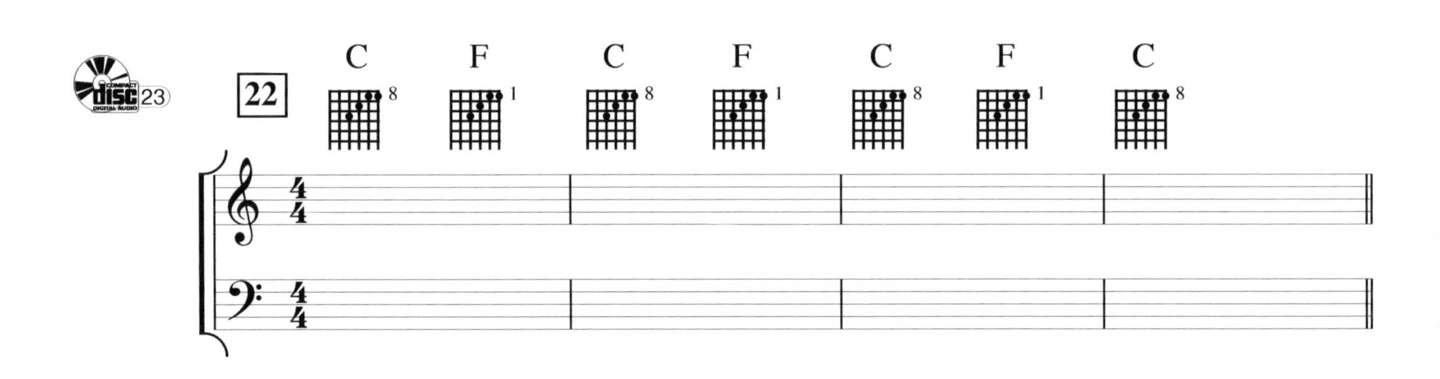

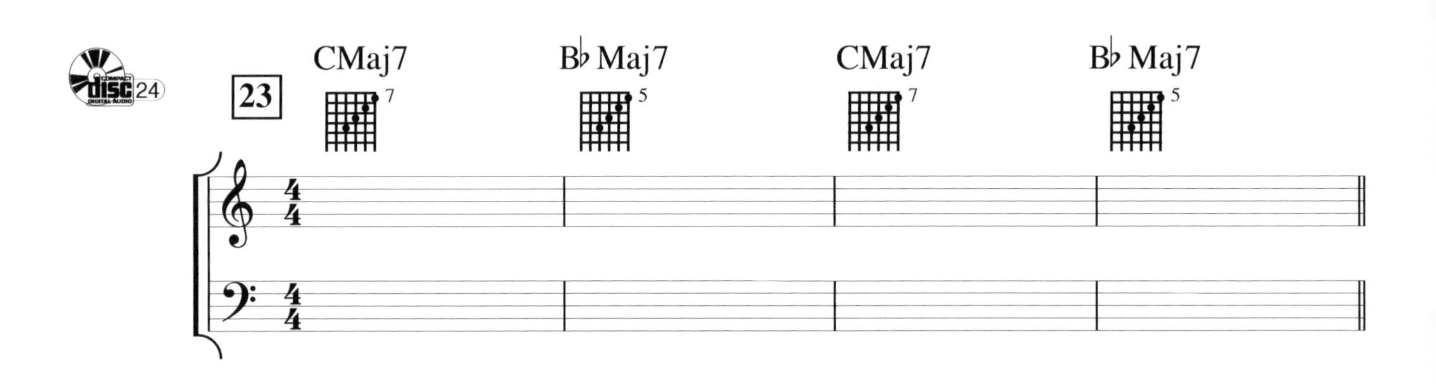

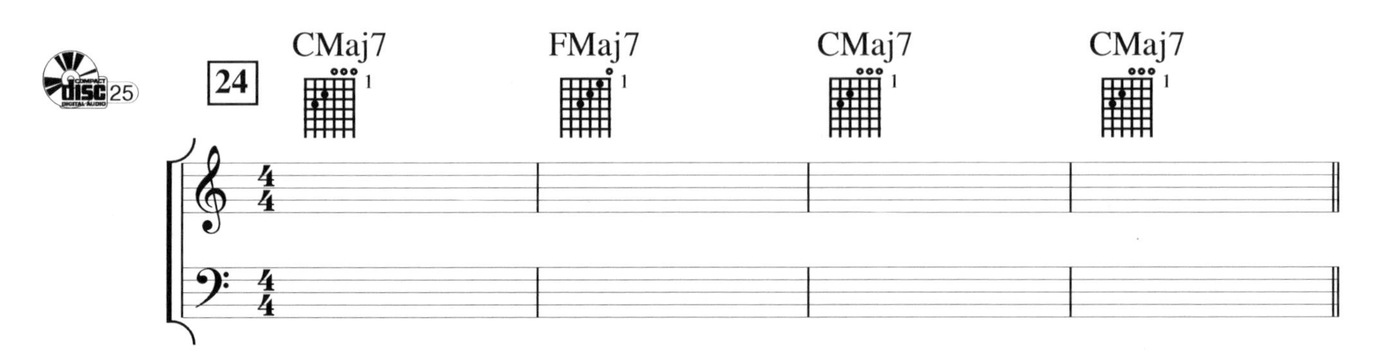

4-Bar Chord Progressions . . . continued

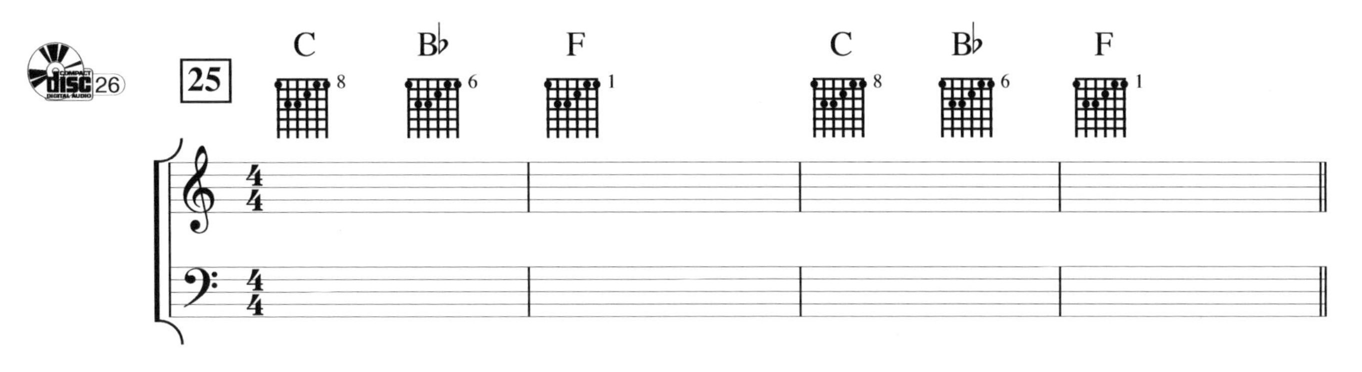

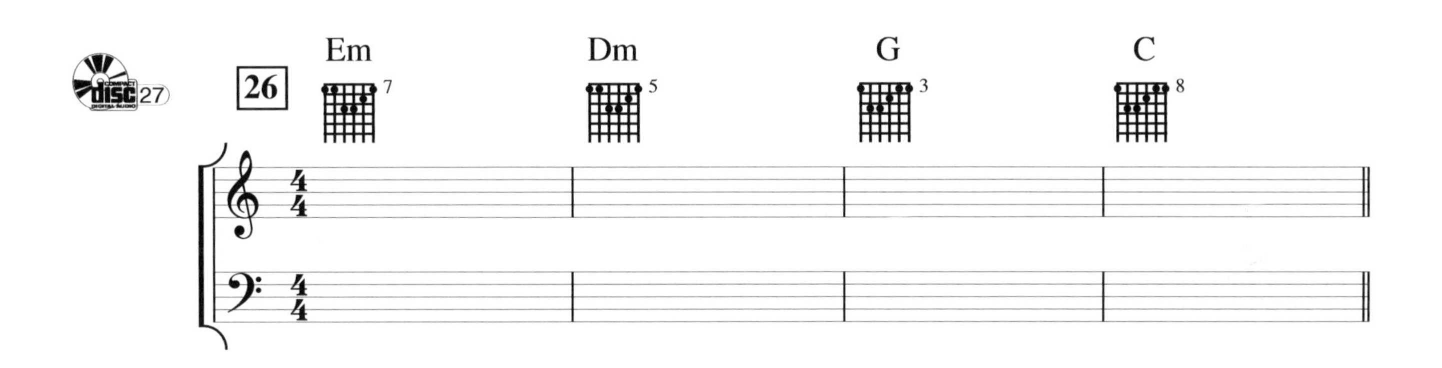

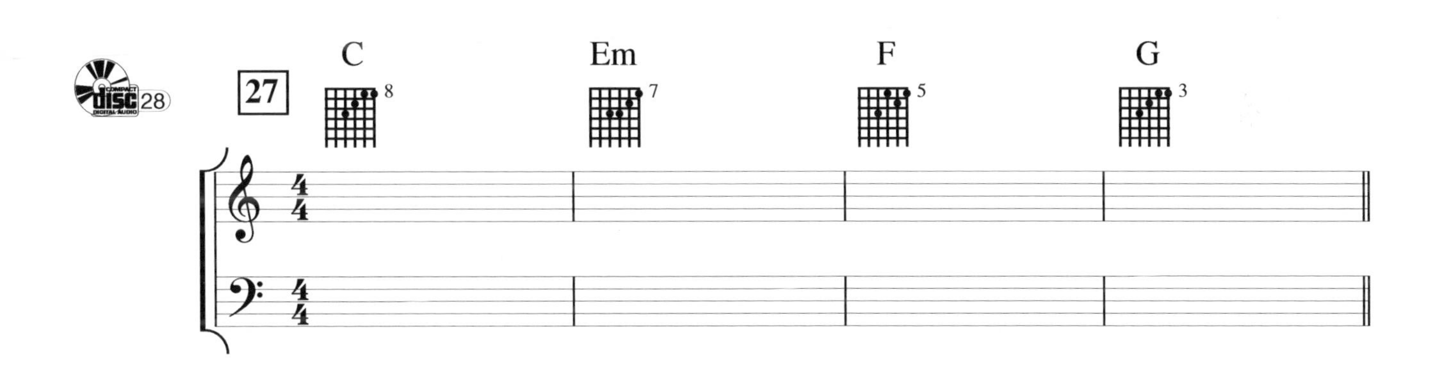

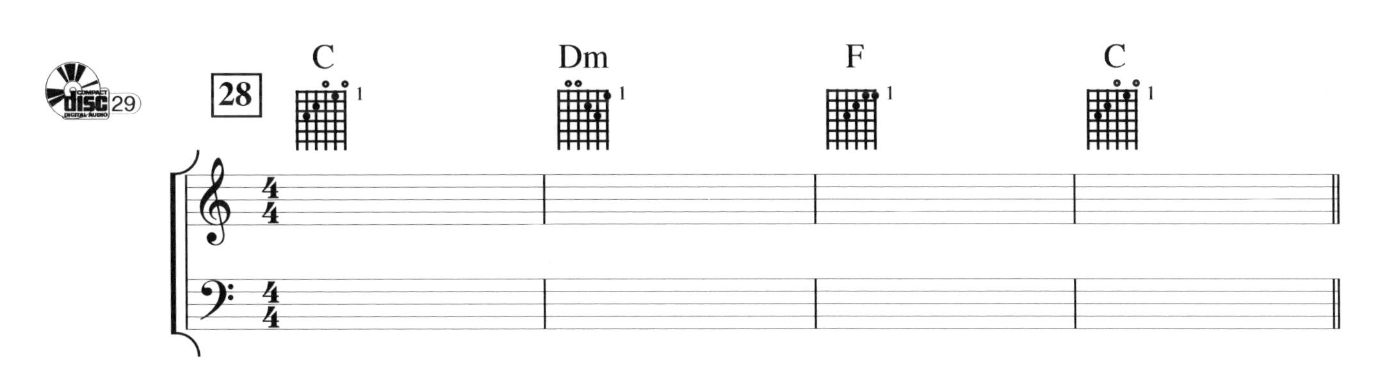

4-Bar Chord Progressions . . . continued

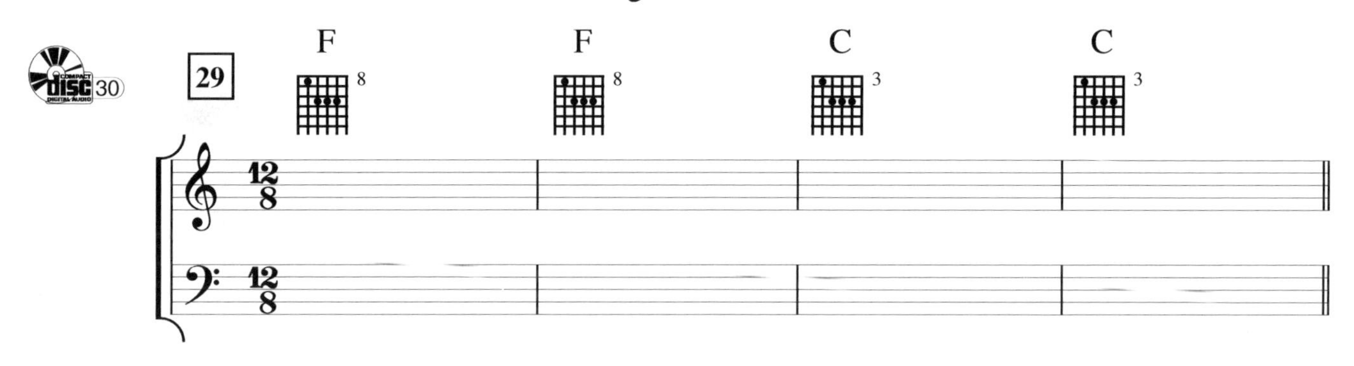

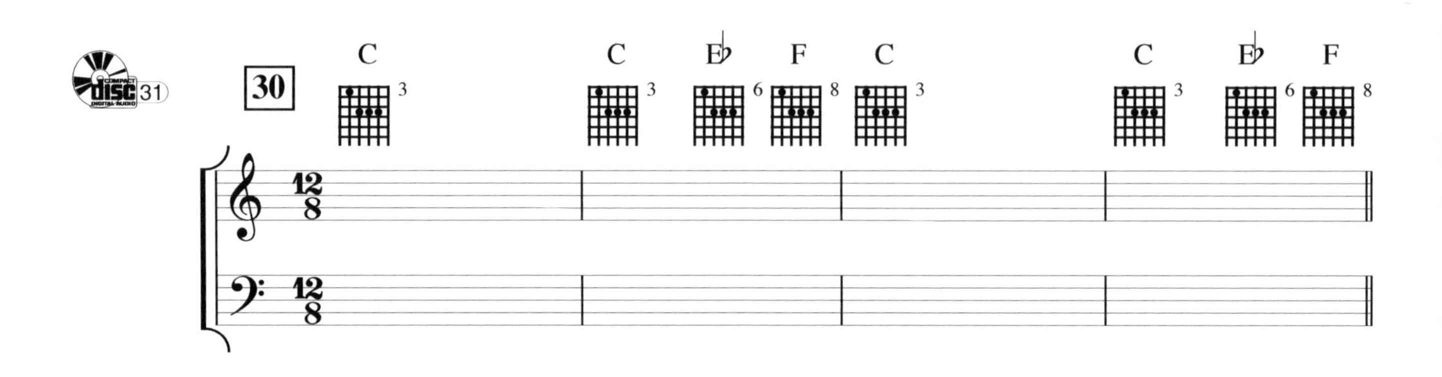

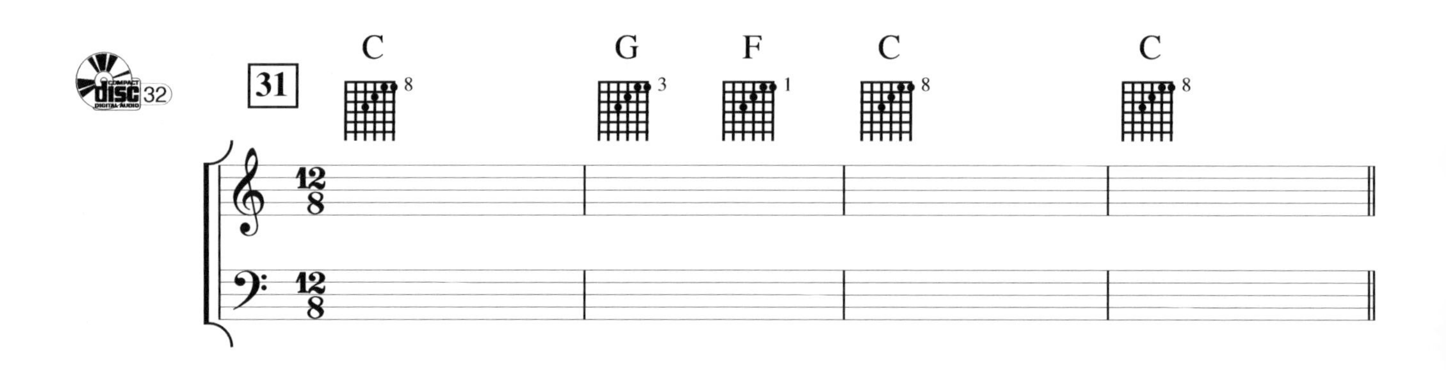

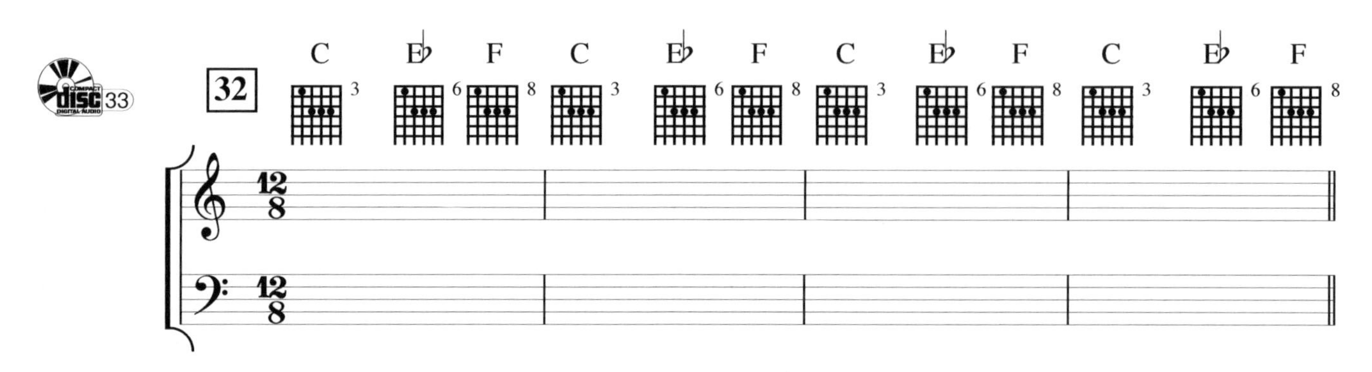

4-Bar Chord Progressions . . . continued

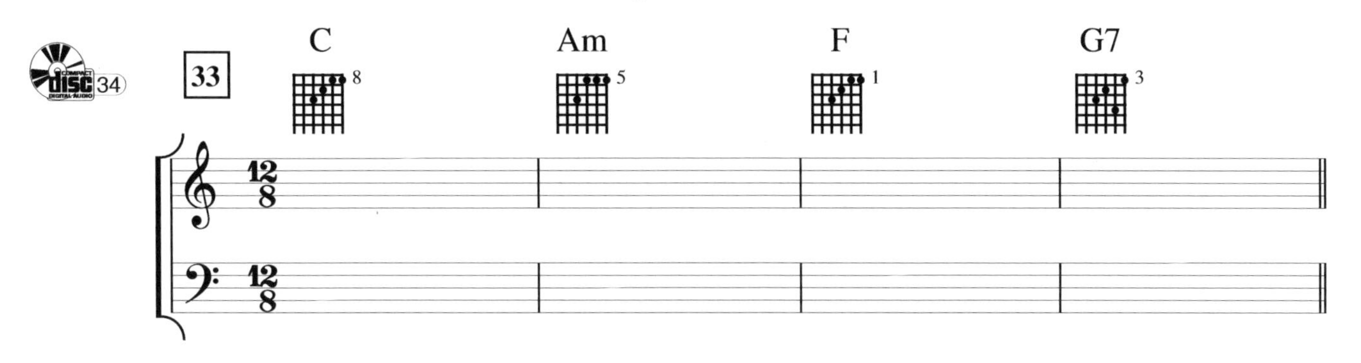

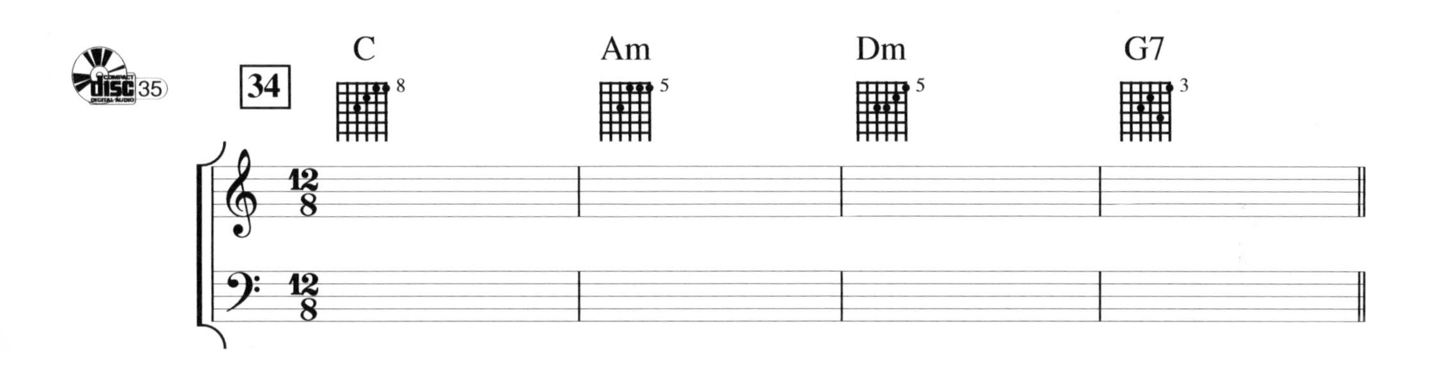

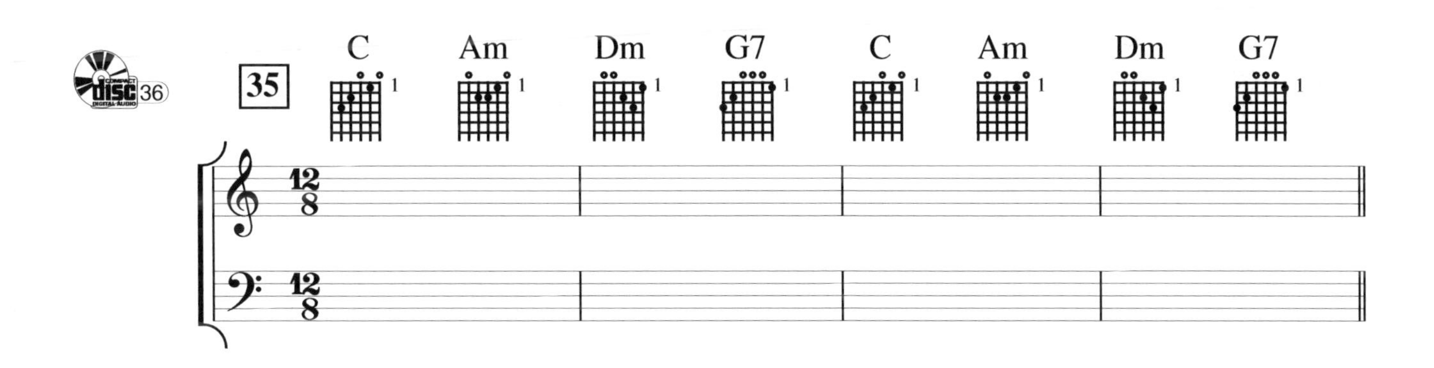

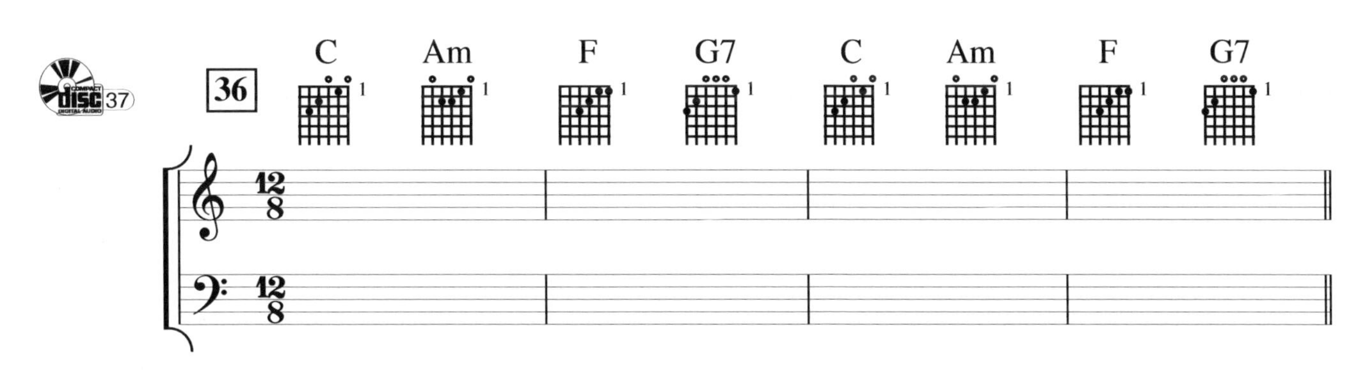

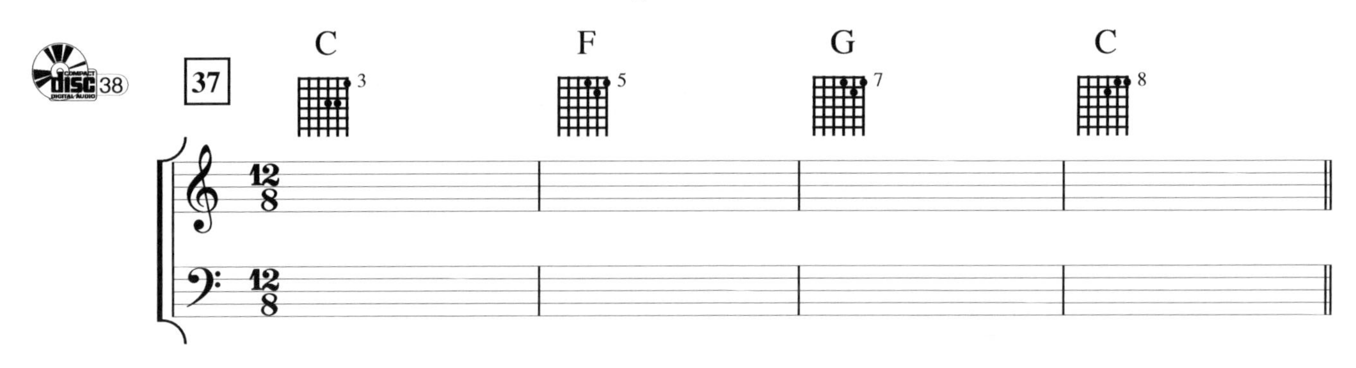
38
37
C
3
F
5
G
7
C
8

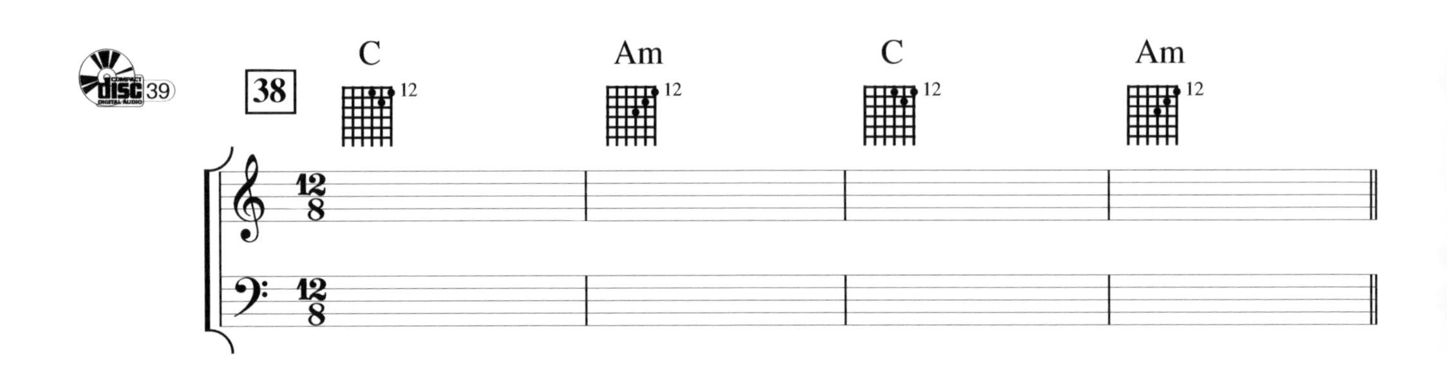
39
38
C
12
Am
12
C
12
Am
12

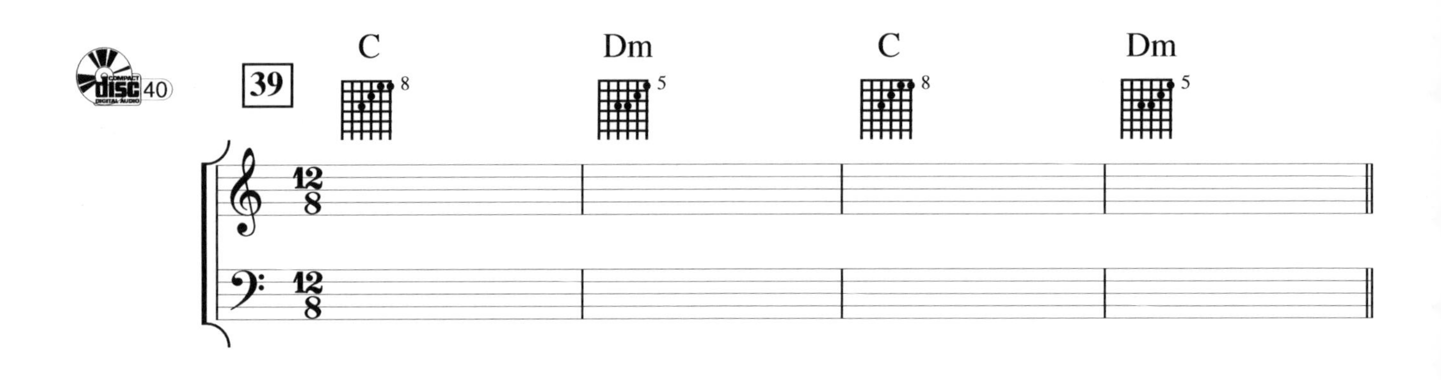
40
39
C
8
Dm
5
C
8
Dm
5

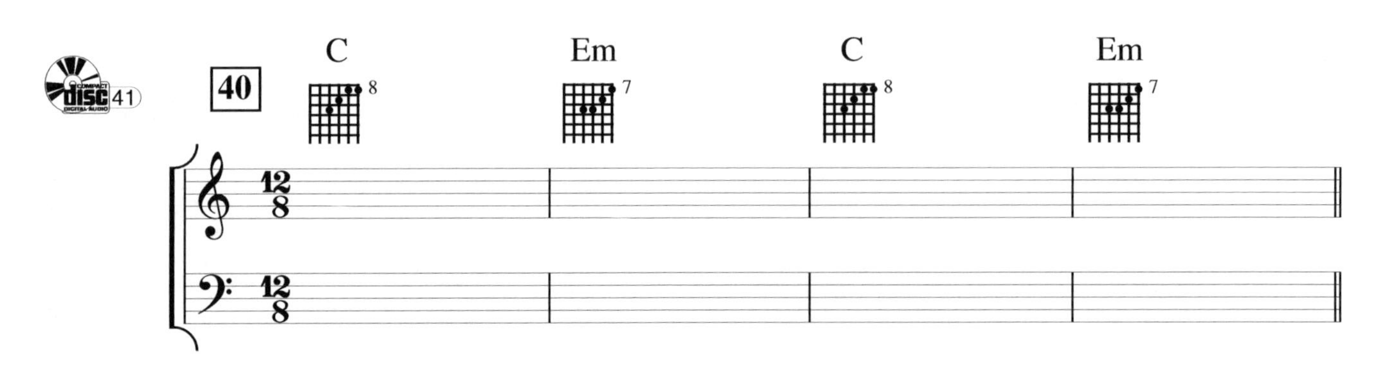
41
40
C
8
Em
7
C
8
Em
7

4-Bar Power Chord Progressions

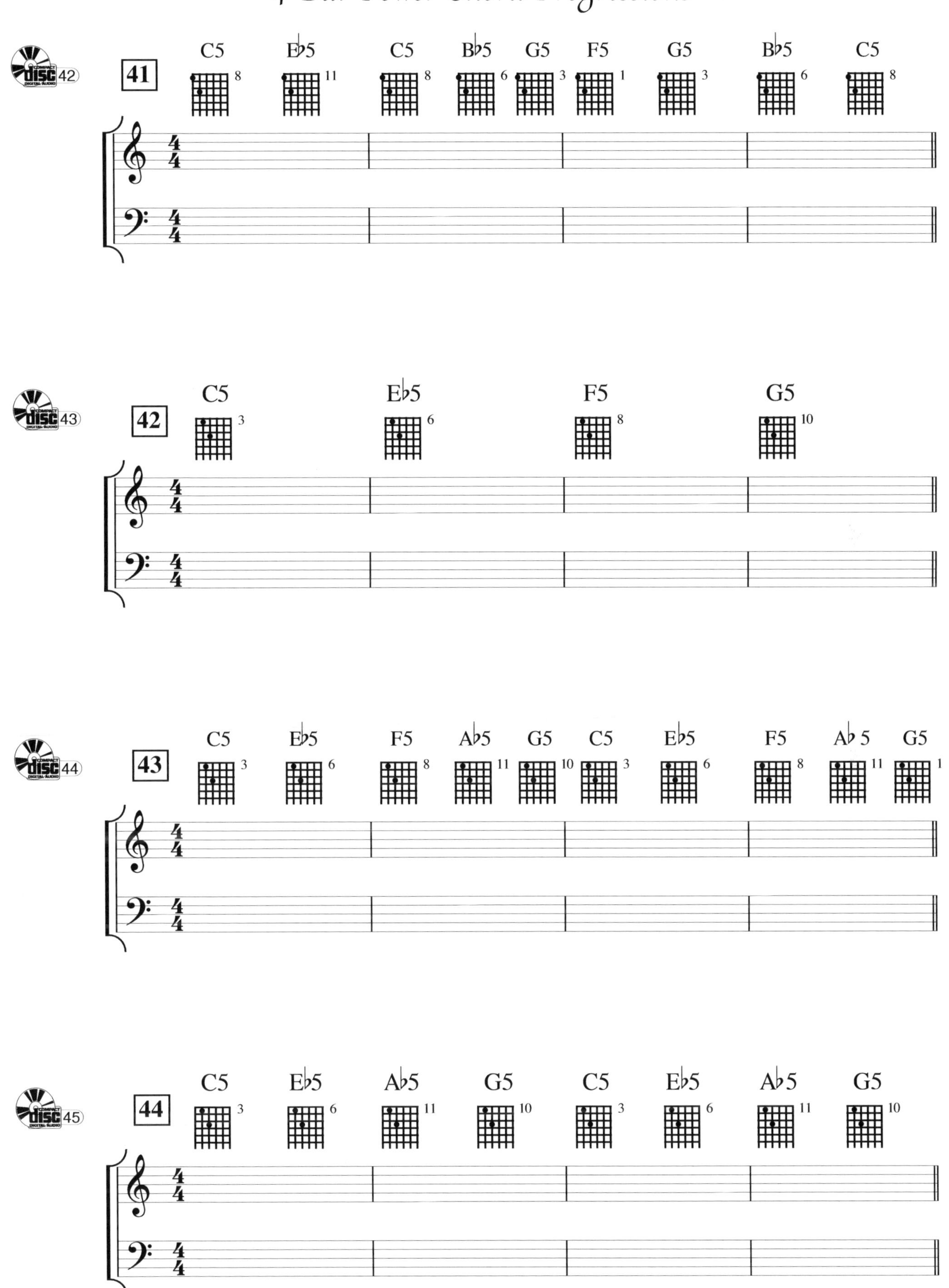

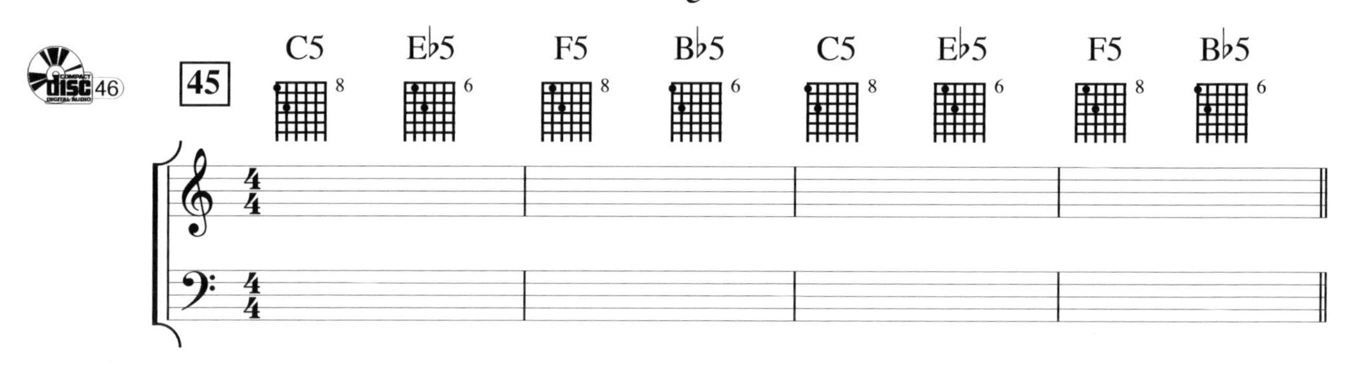
46
45
C5 8
E♭5 6
F5 8
B♭5 6
C5 8
E♭5 6
F5 8
B♭5 6

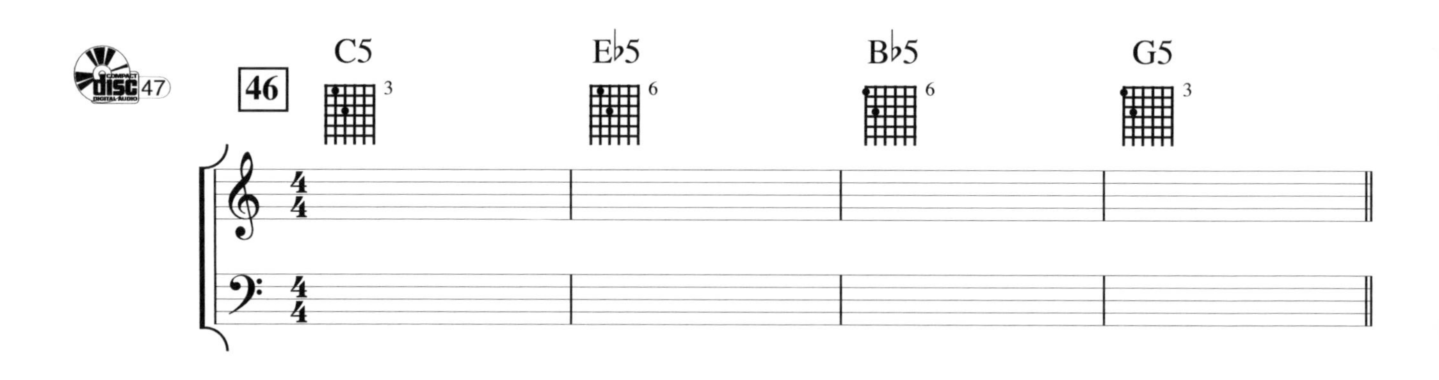
47
46
C5 3
E♭5 6
B♭5 6
G5 3

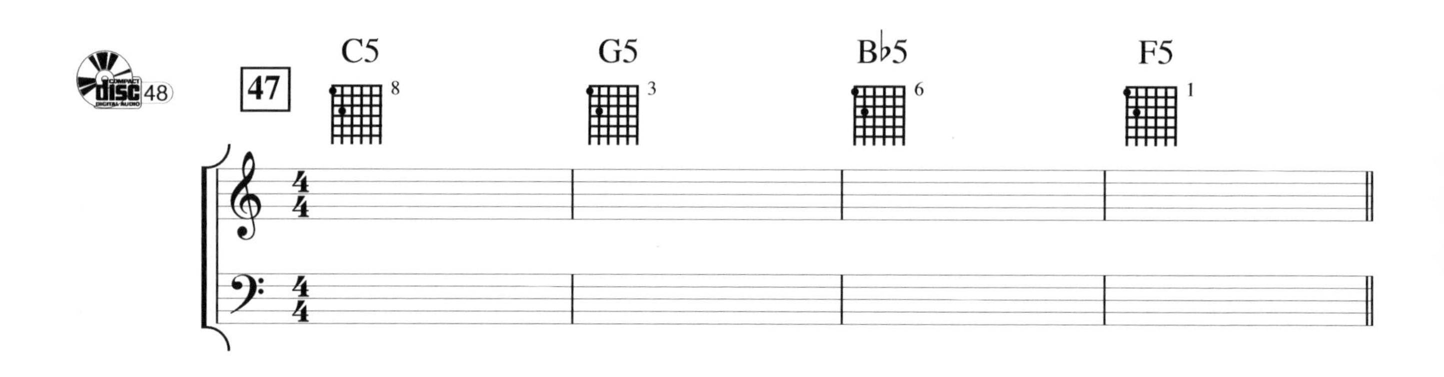
48
47
C5 8
G5 3
B♭5 6
F5 1

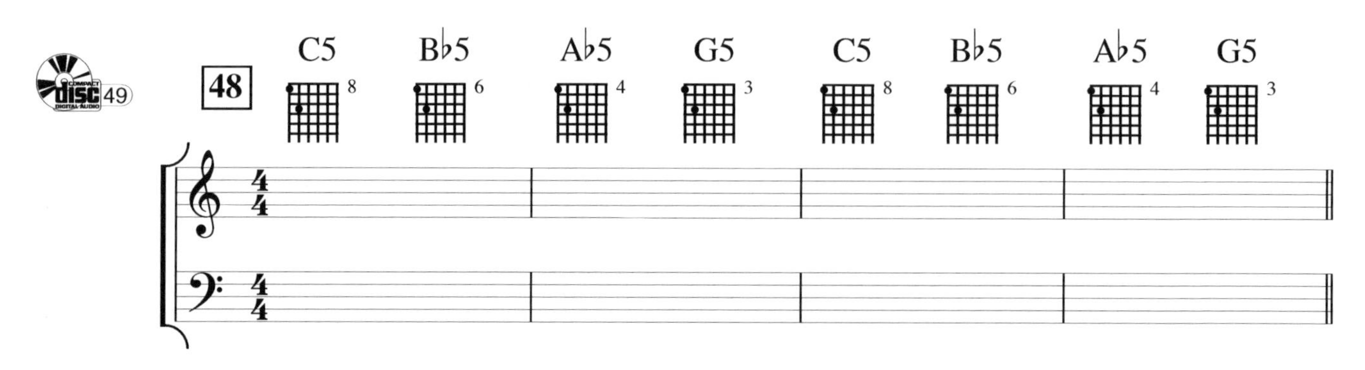
49
48
C5 8
B♭5 6
A♭5 4
G5 3
C5 8
B♭5 6
A♭5 4
G5 3

4-Bar Power Chord Progressions . . . continued

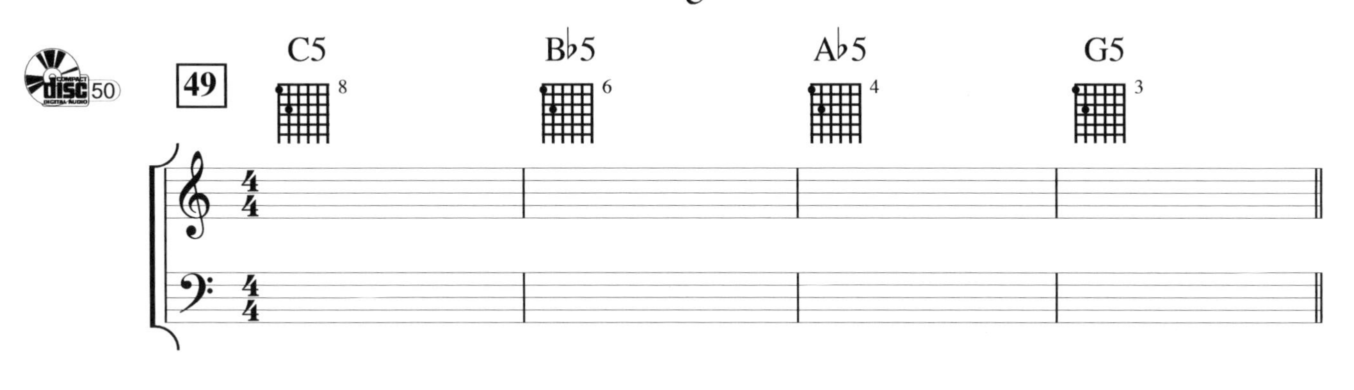

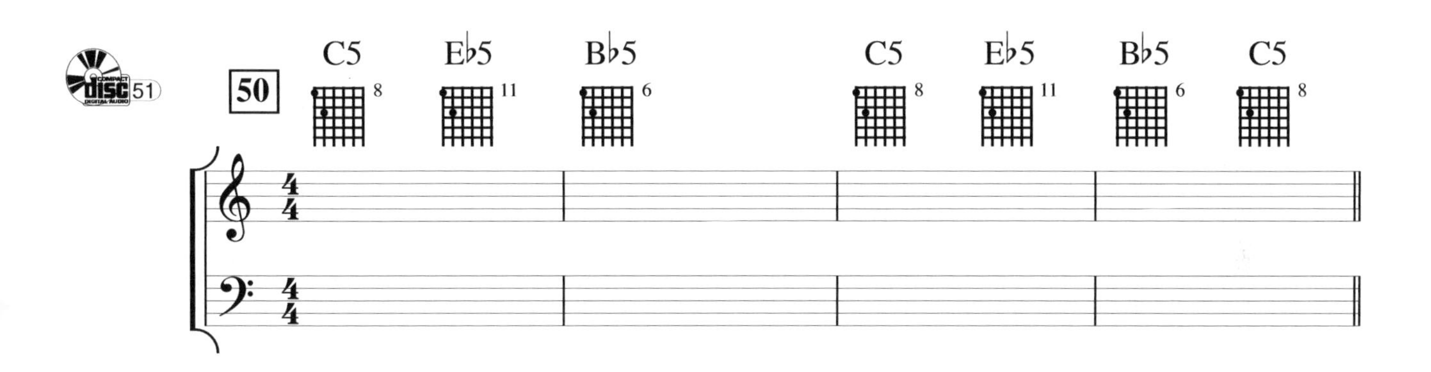

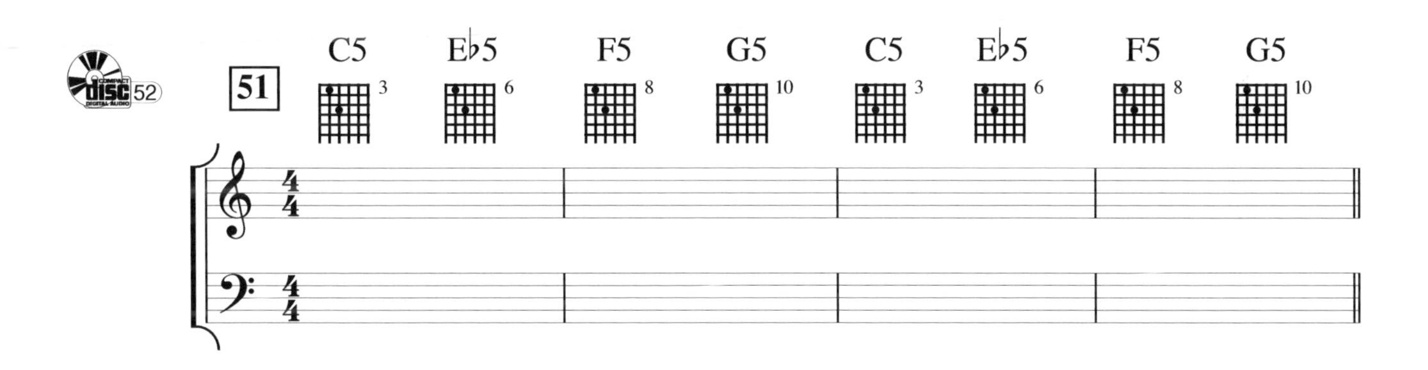

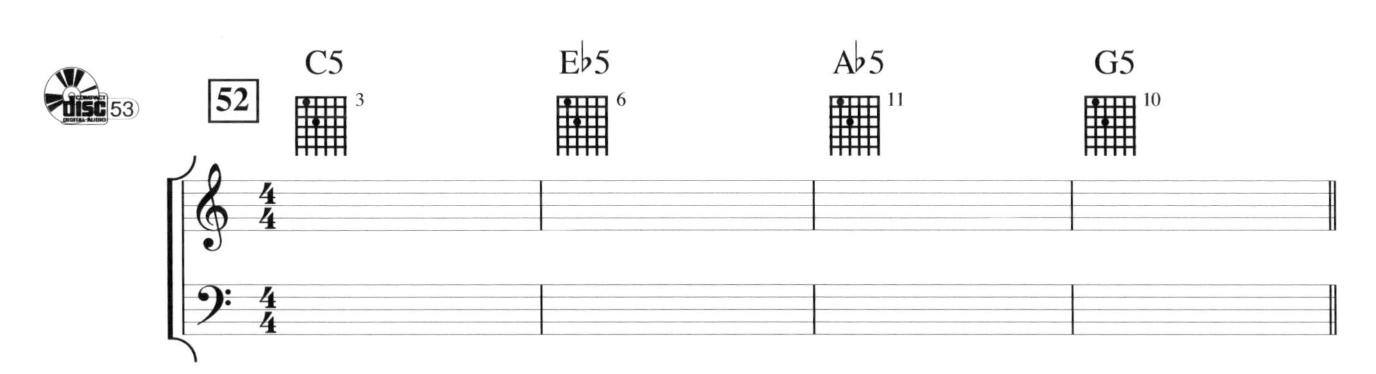

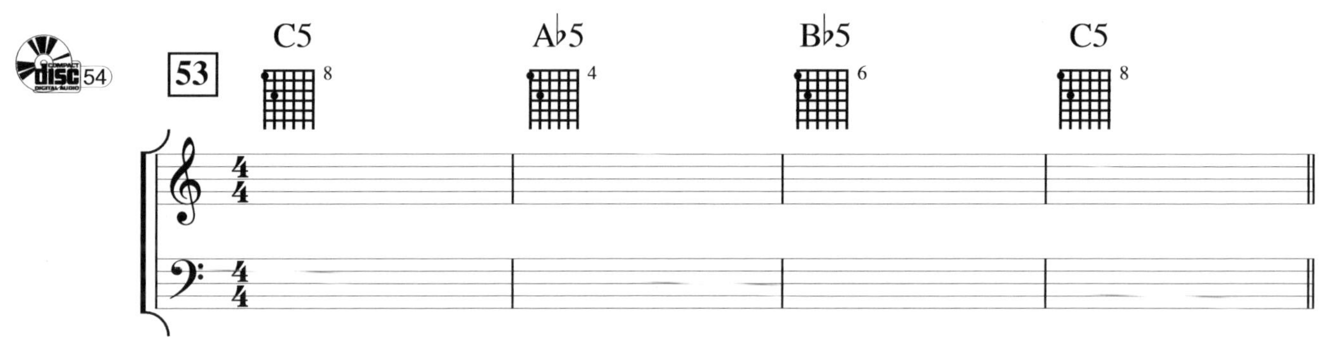

Example 53 is played on CD track 54, part one.

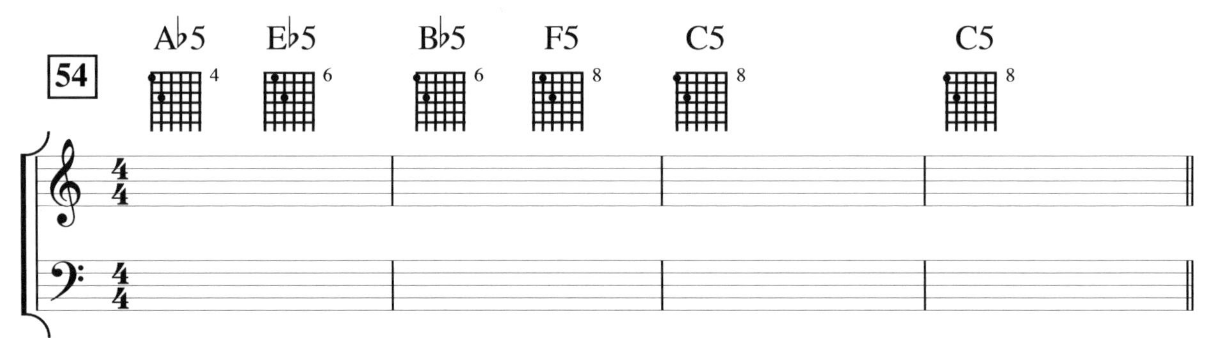

Example 54 is played on CD track 54, part two.

8-Bar Chord Progressions

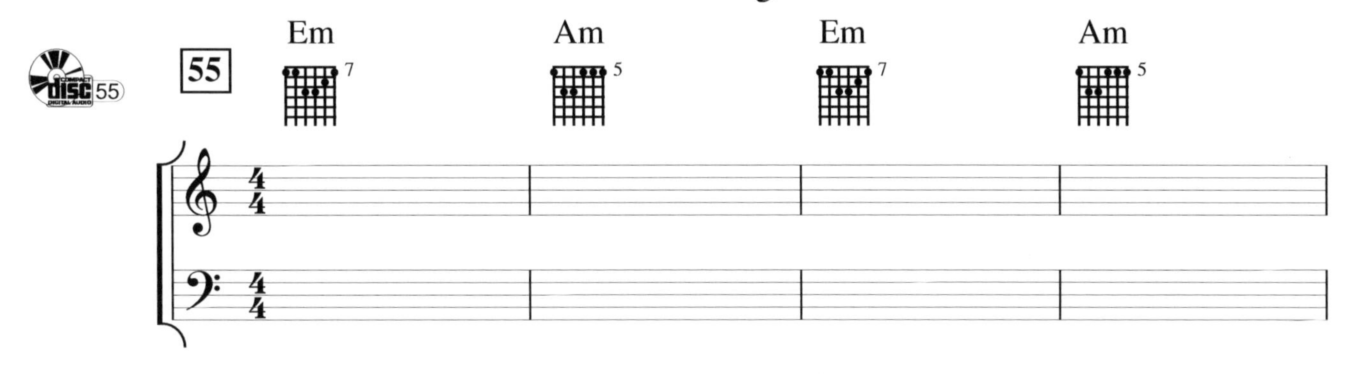

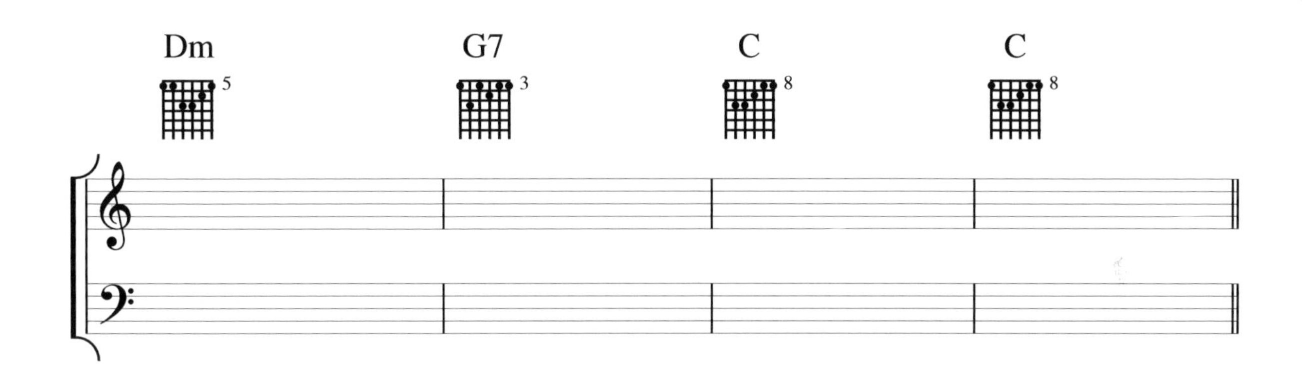

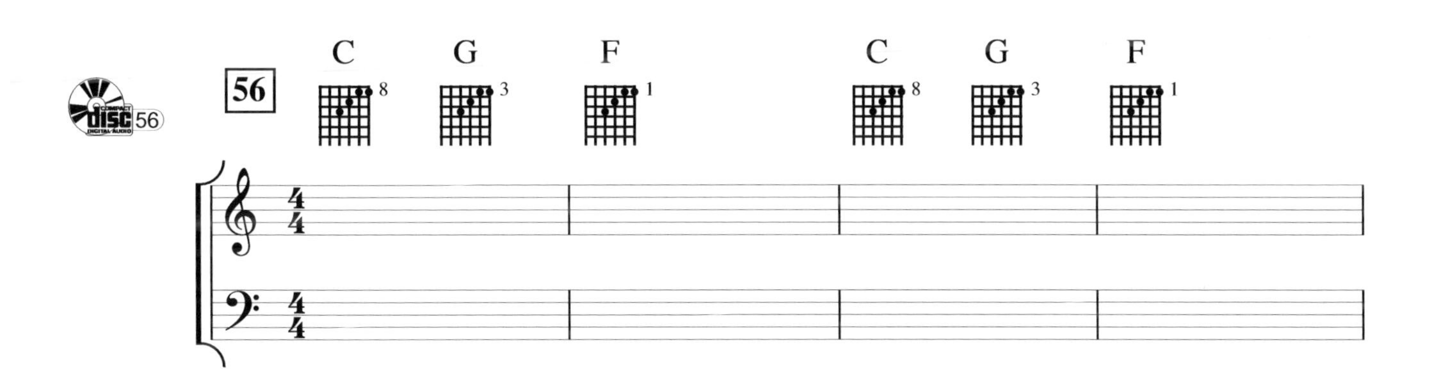

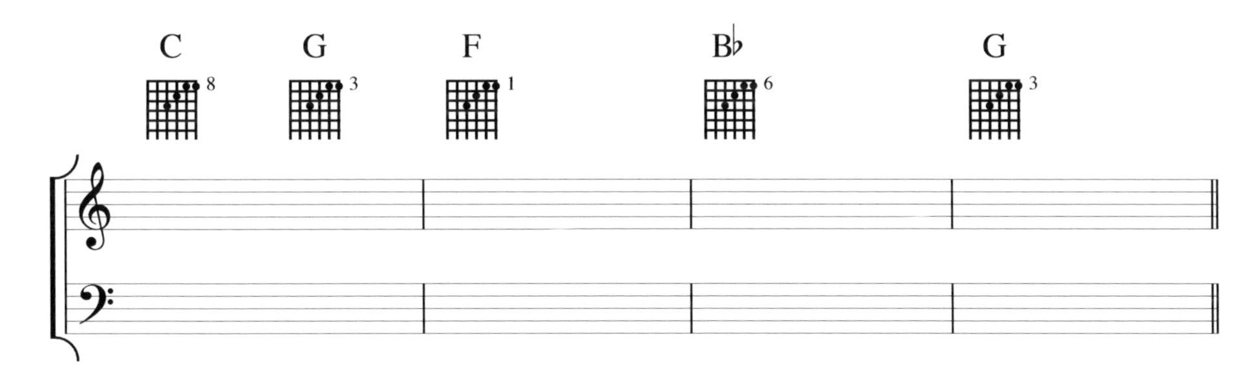

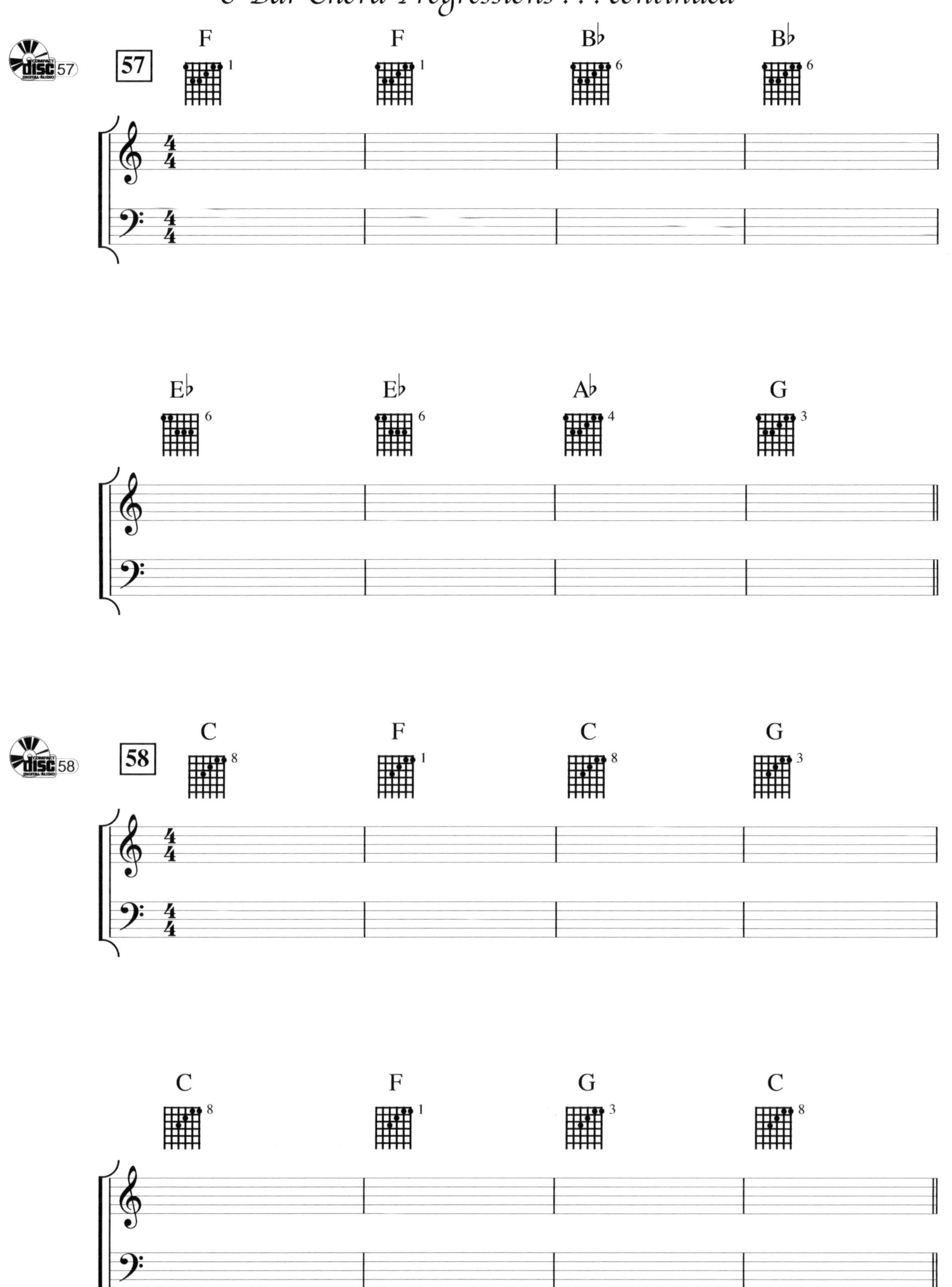
57
57
F
1
F
1
B♭
6
B♭
6
E♭
6
E♭
6
A♭
4
G
3
58
58
C
8
F
1
C
8
G
3
C
8
F
1
G
3
C
8

8-Bar Chord Progressions . . . continued

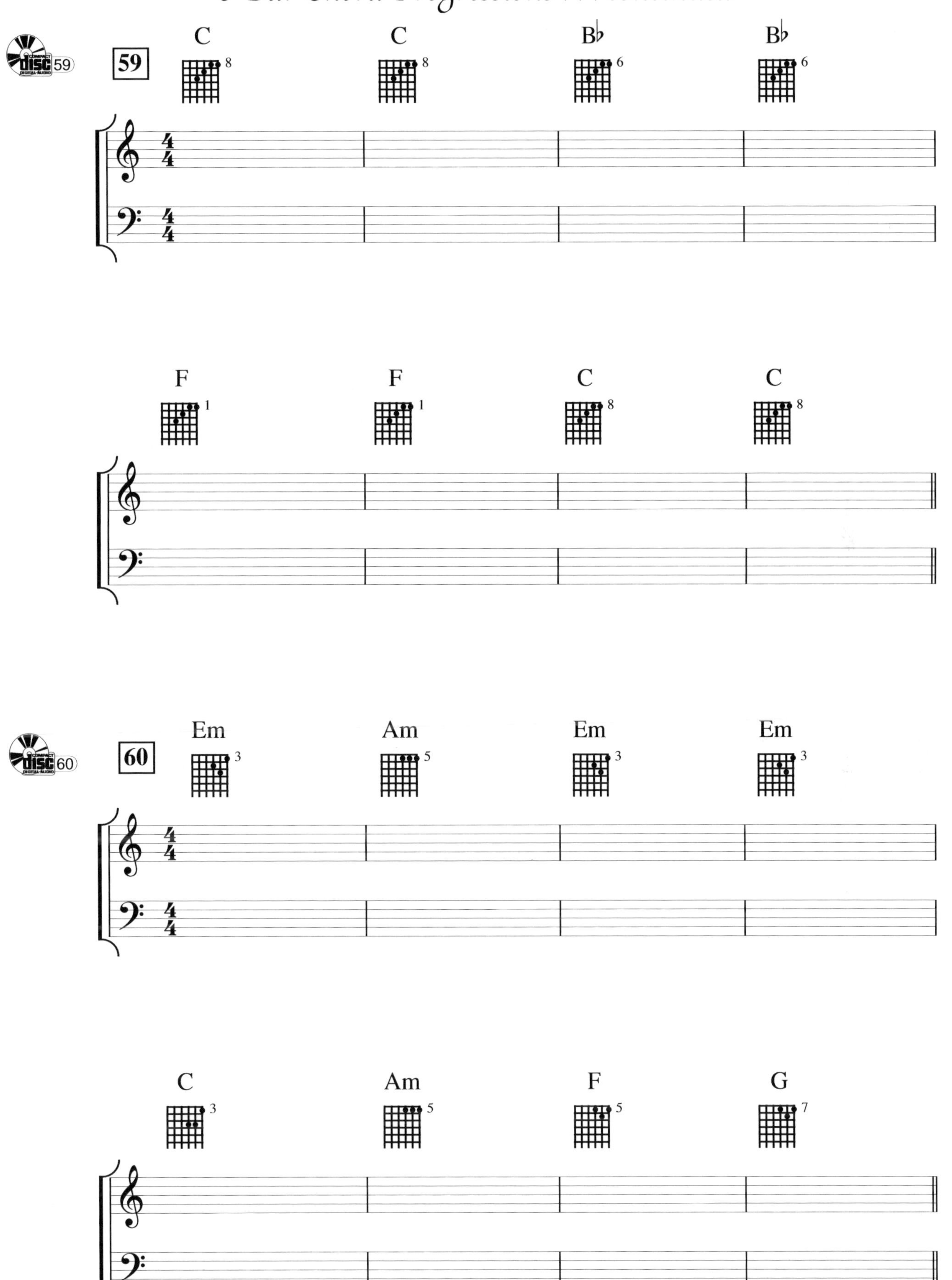

8-Bar Chord Progressions . . . continued

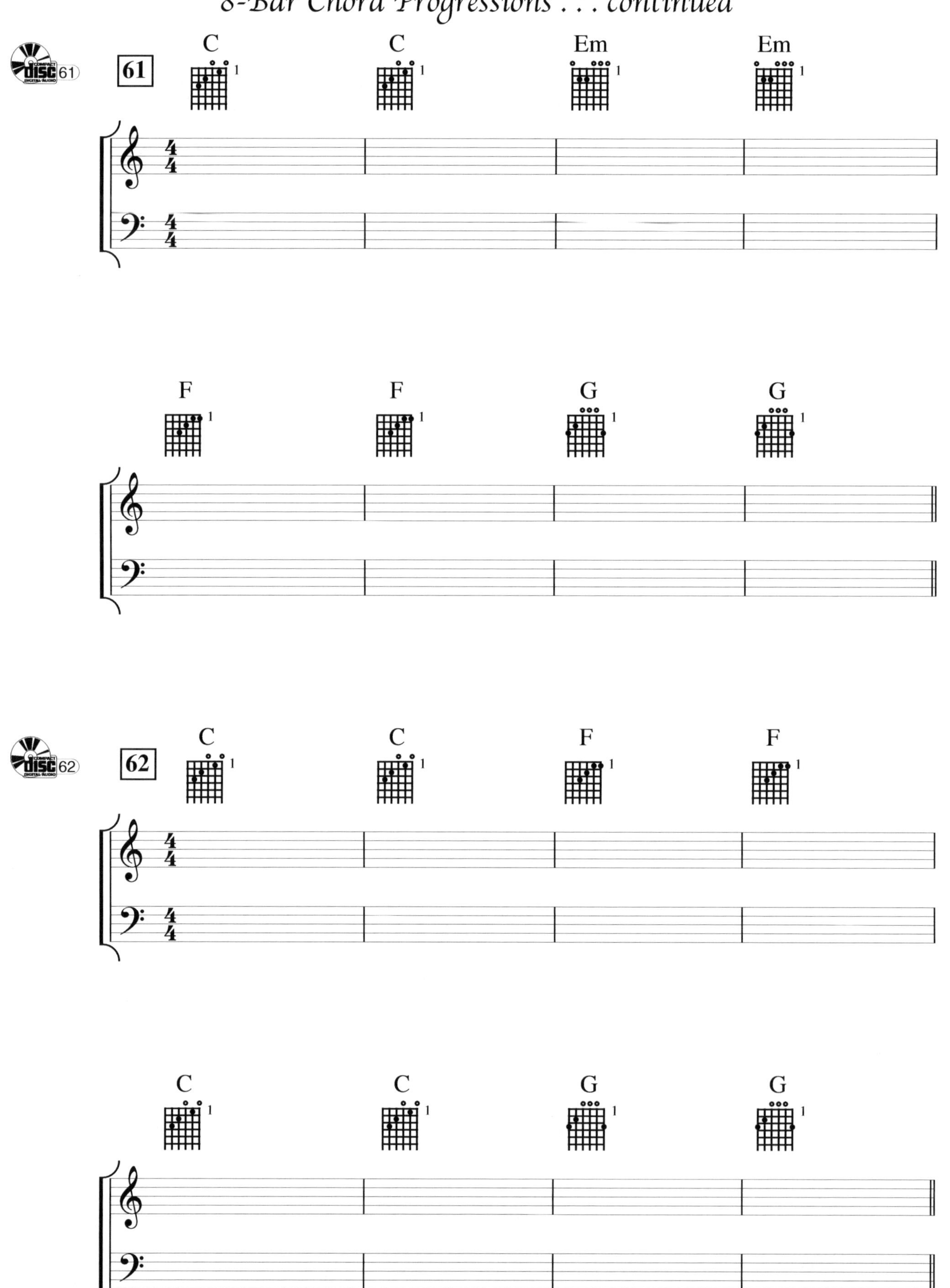

8-Bar Chord Progressions . . . continued

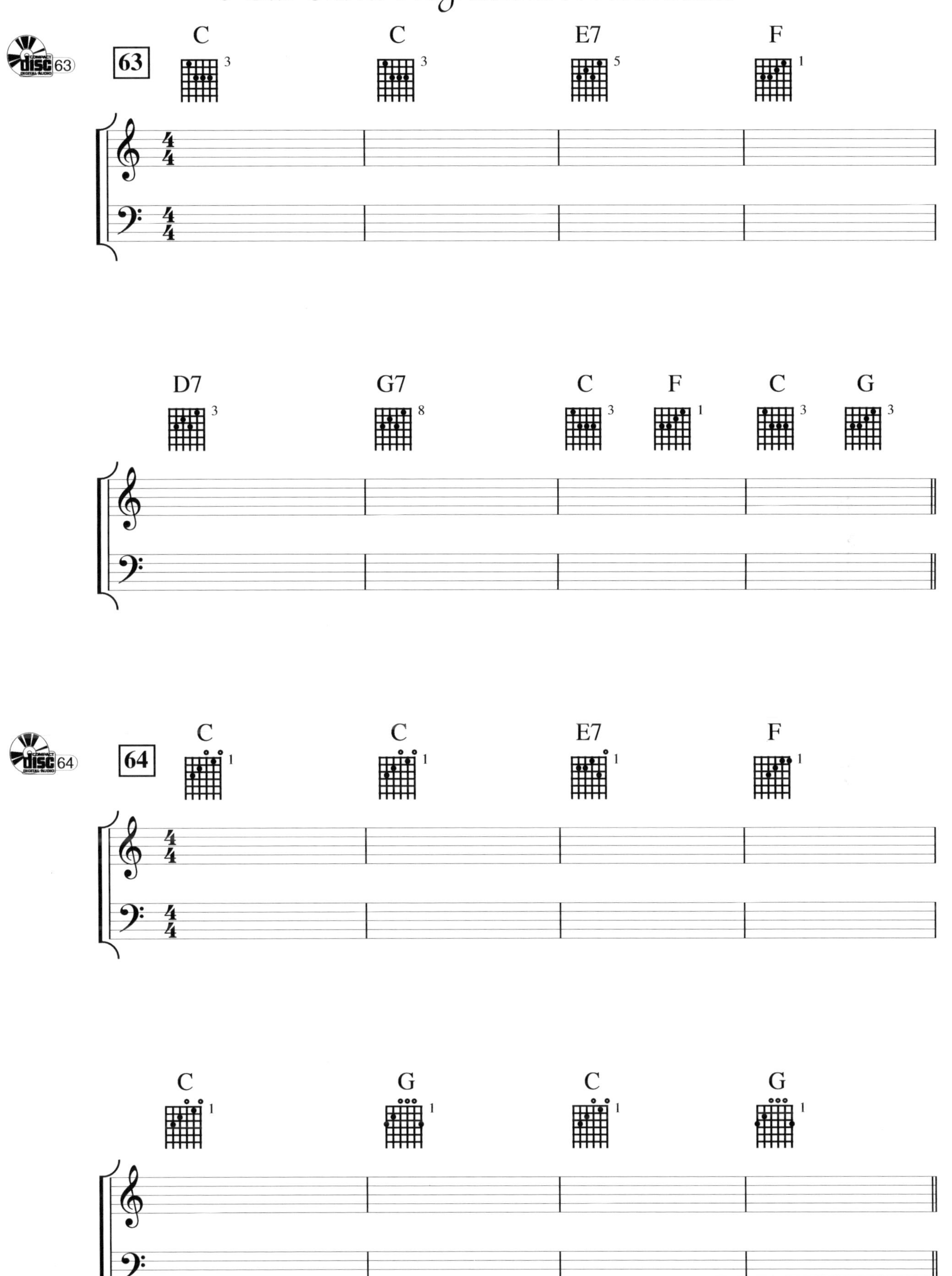

8-Bar Chord Progressions . . . continued

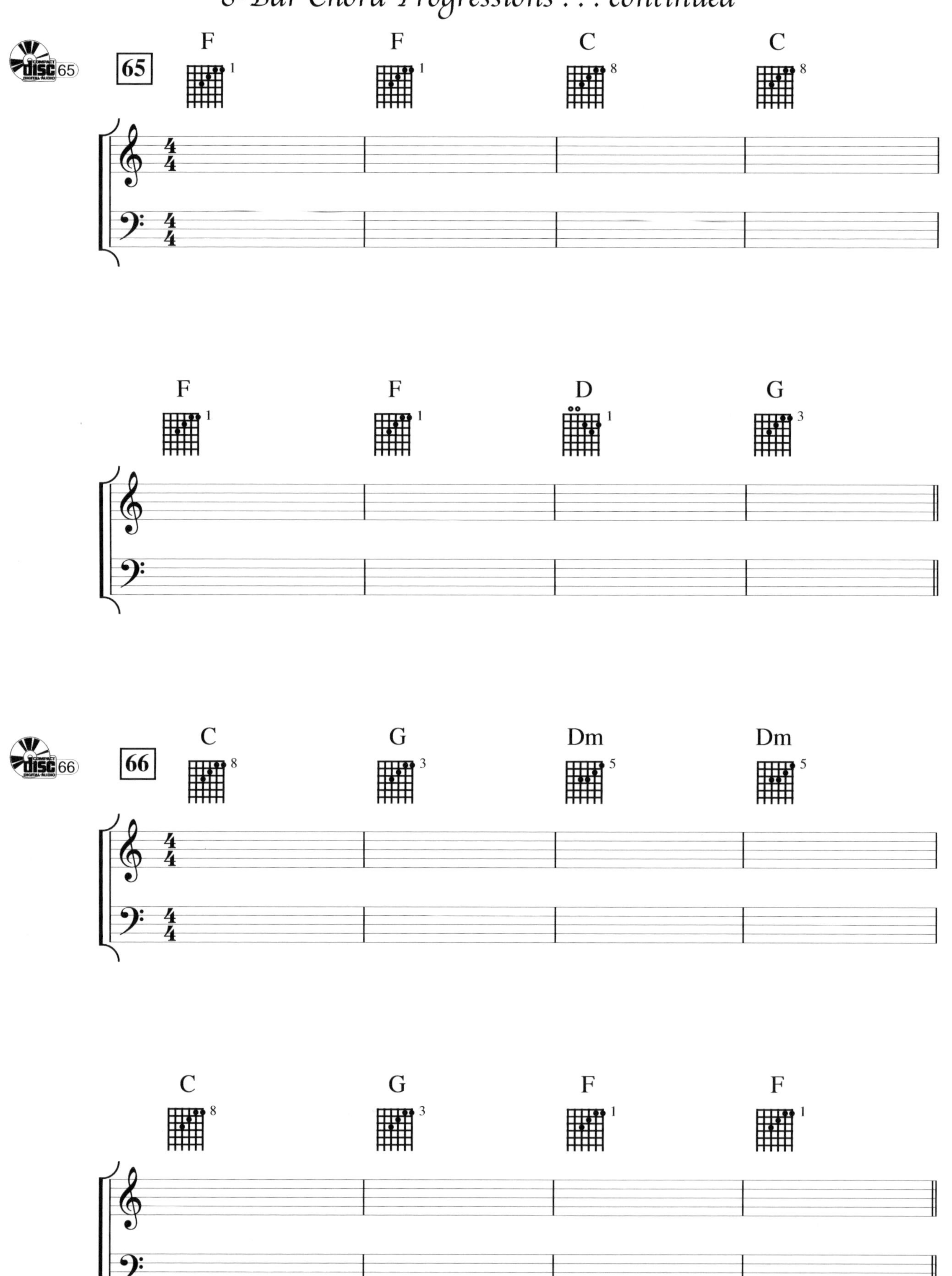

8-Bar Chord Progressions . . . continued

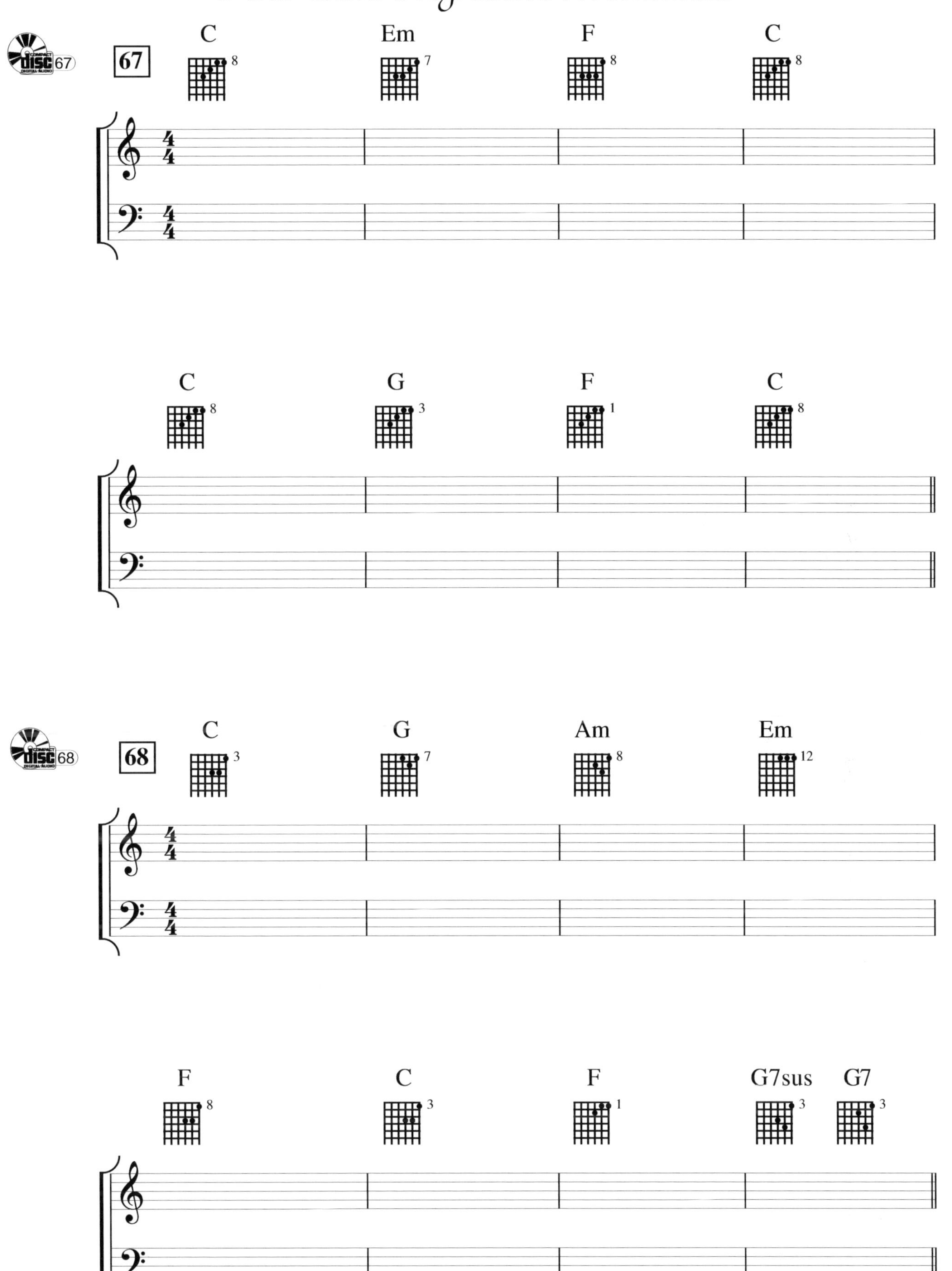

8-Bar Chord Progressions . . . continued

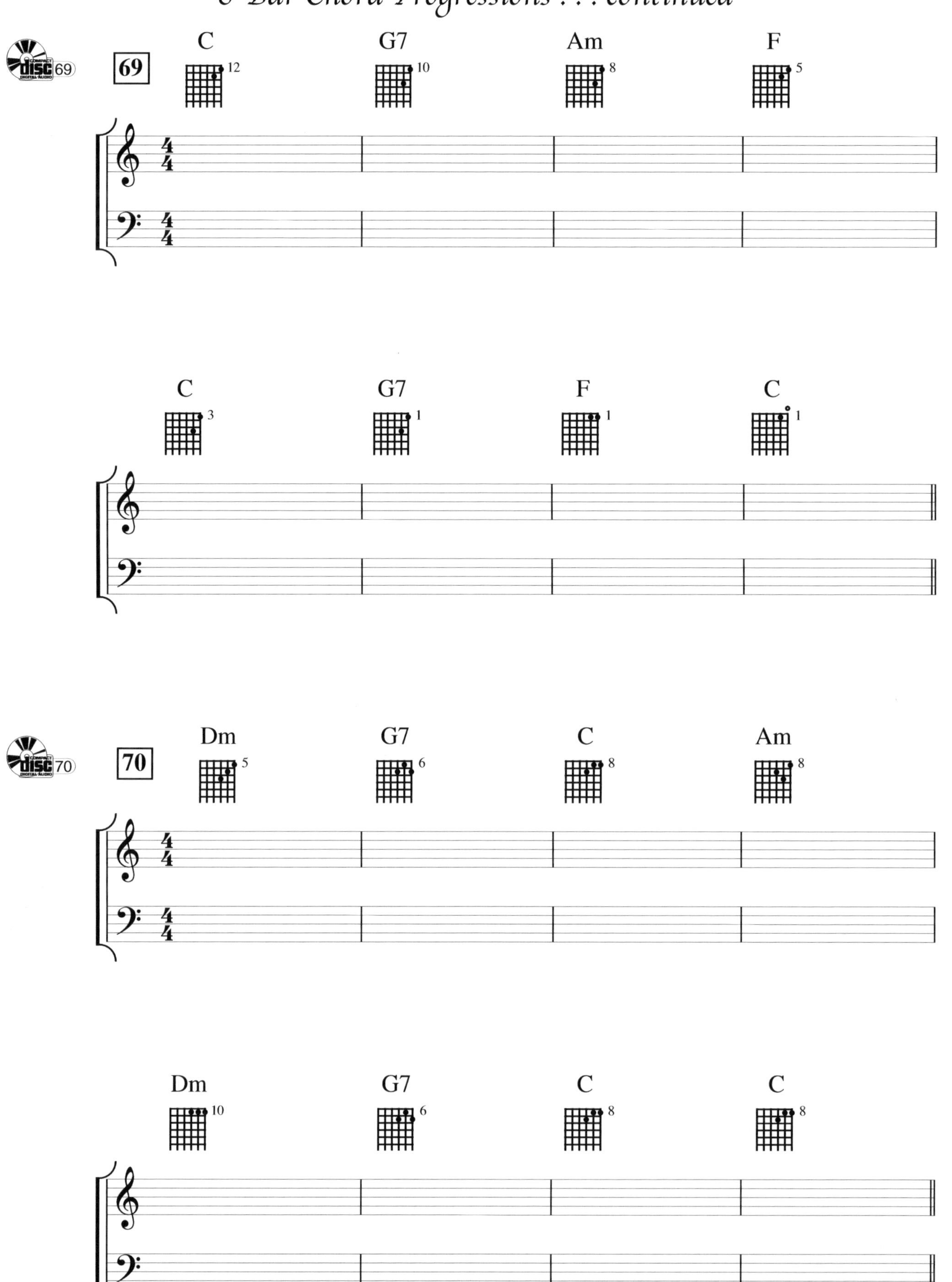

8-Bar Chord Progressions . . . continued

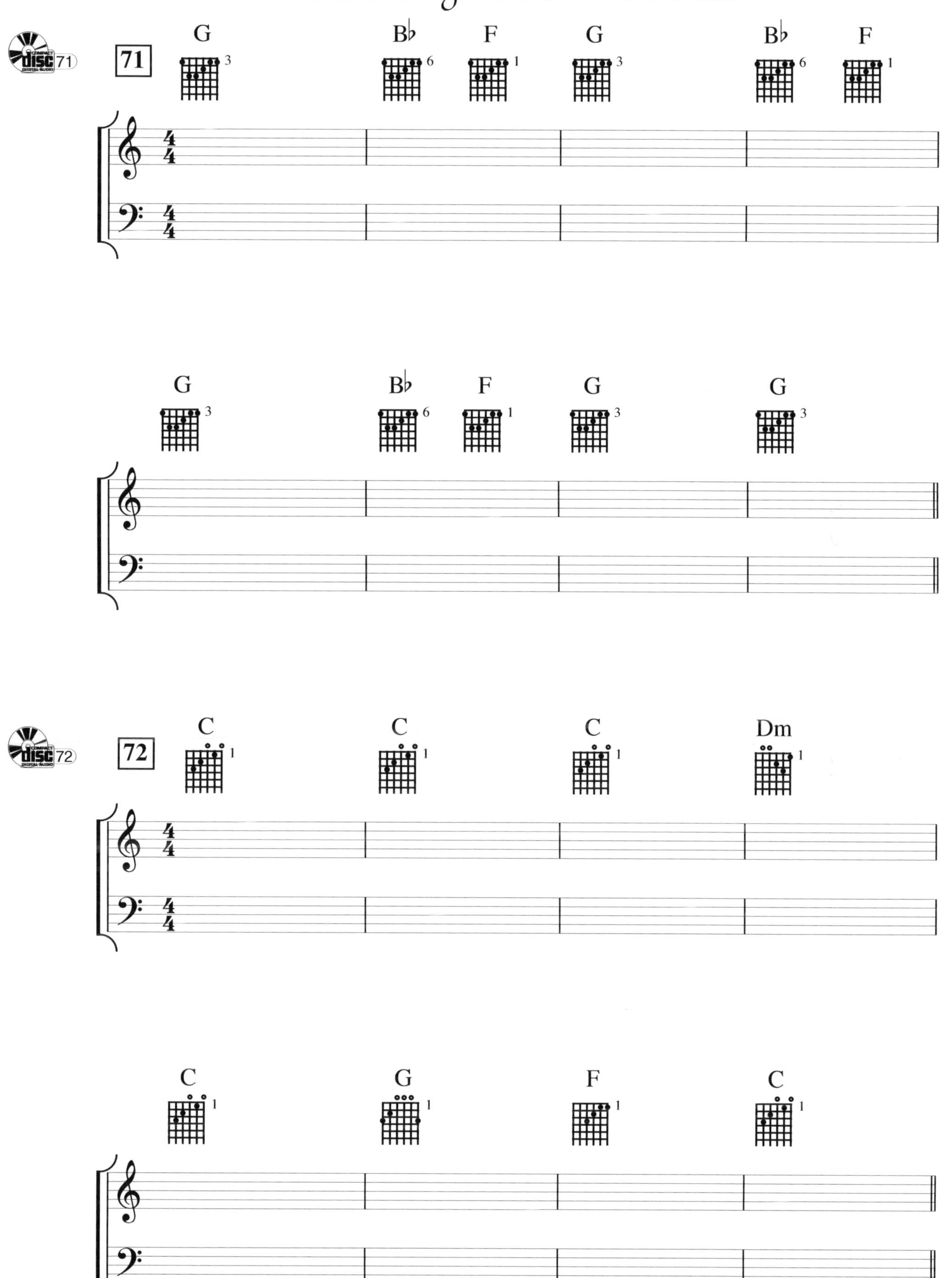

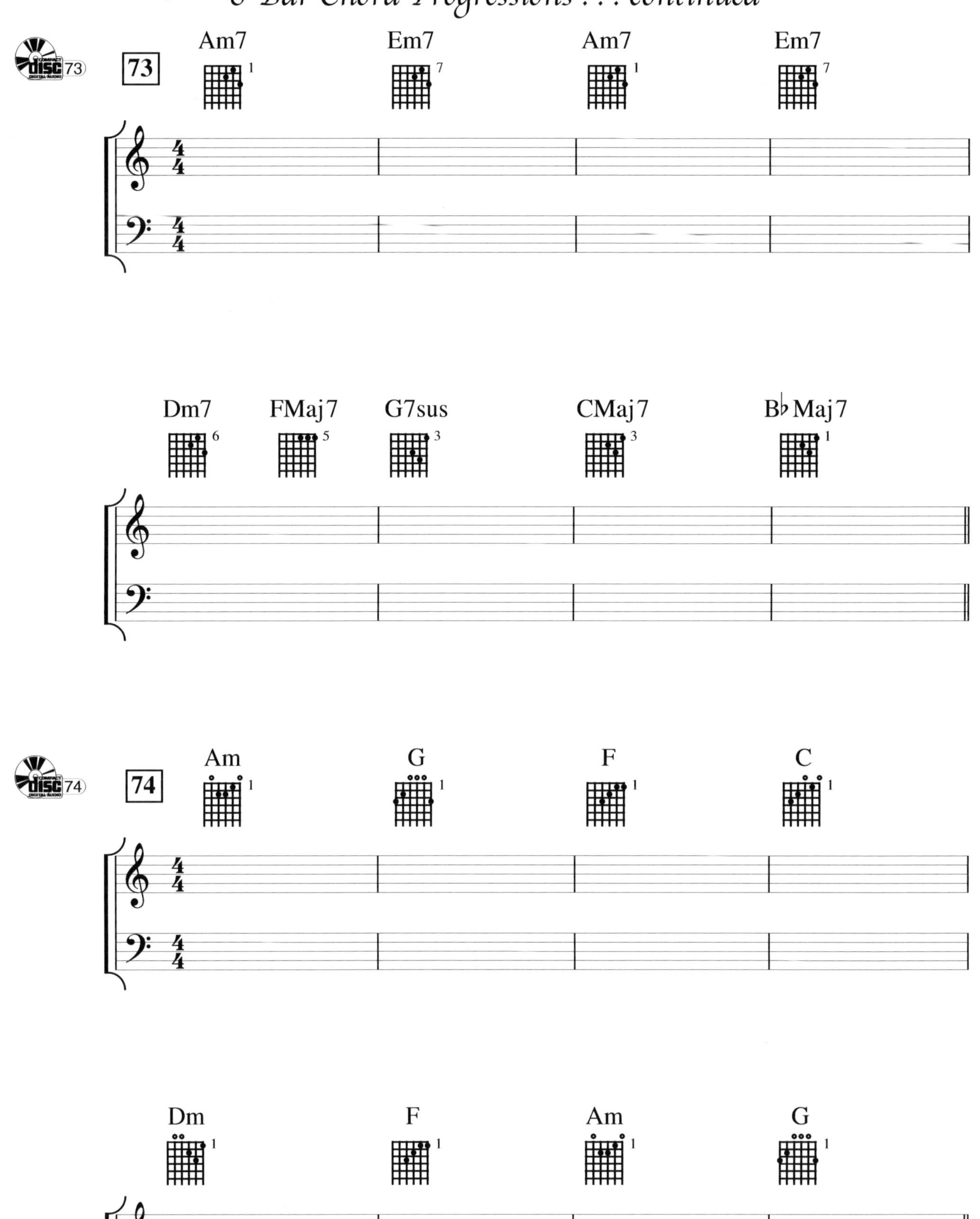

73
73
Am7
1
Em7
7
Am7
1
Em7
7
Dm7
6
FMaj7
5
G7sus
3
CMaj7
3
B♭Maj7
1
74
74
Am
1
G
1
F
1
C
1
Dm
1
F
1
Am
1
G
1

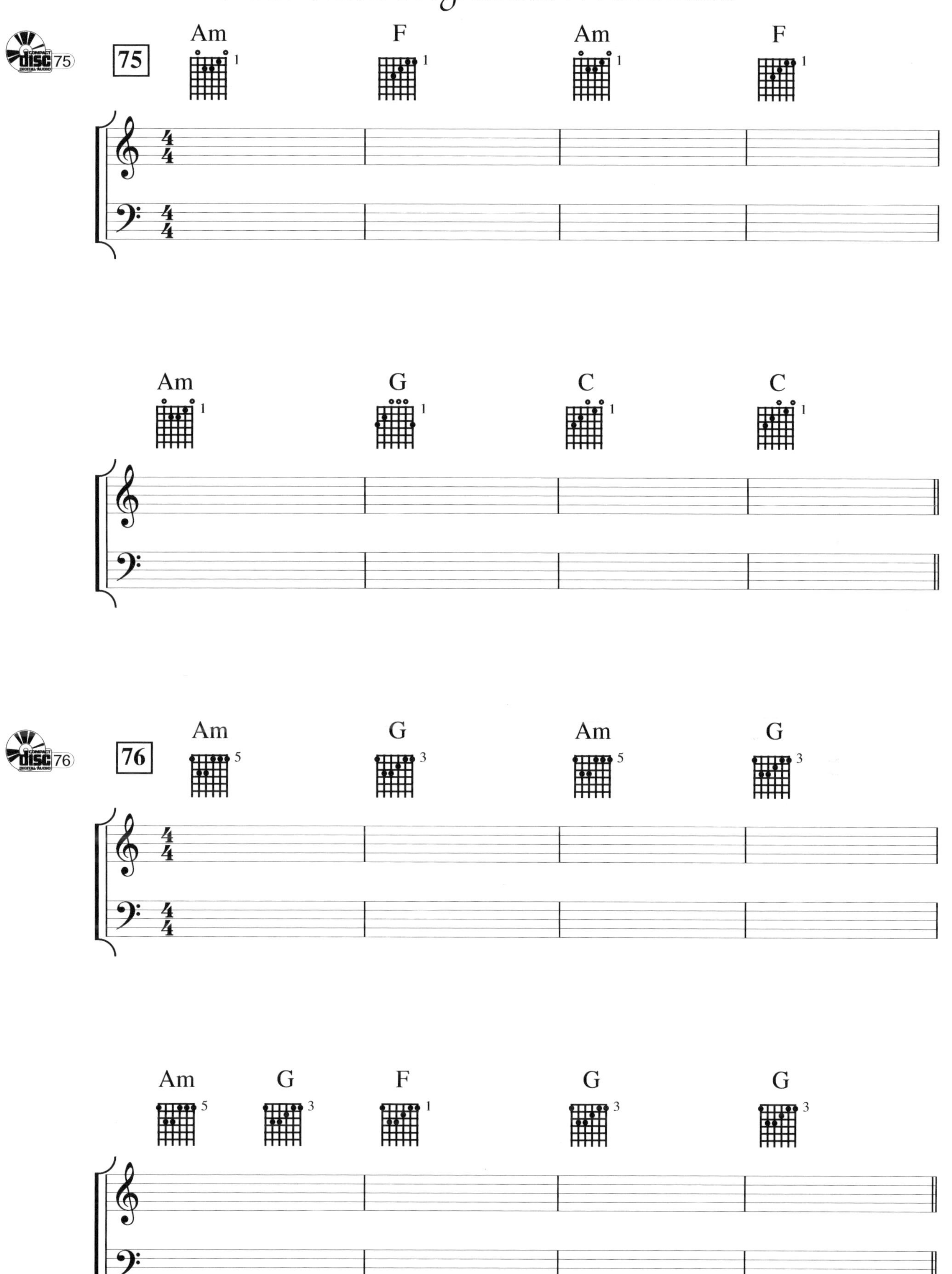
75
Am
F
Am
F
Am
G
C
C
76
Am
G
Am
G
Am
G
F
G
G

8-Bar Chord Progressions . . . continued

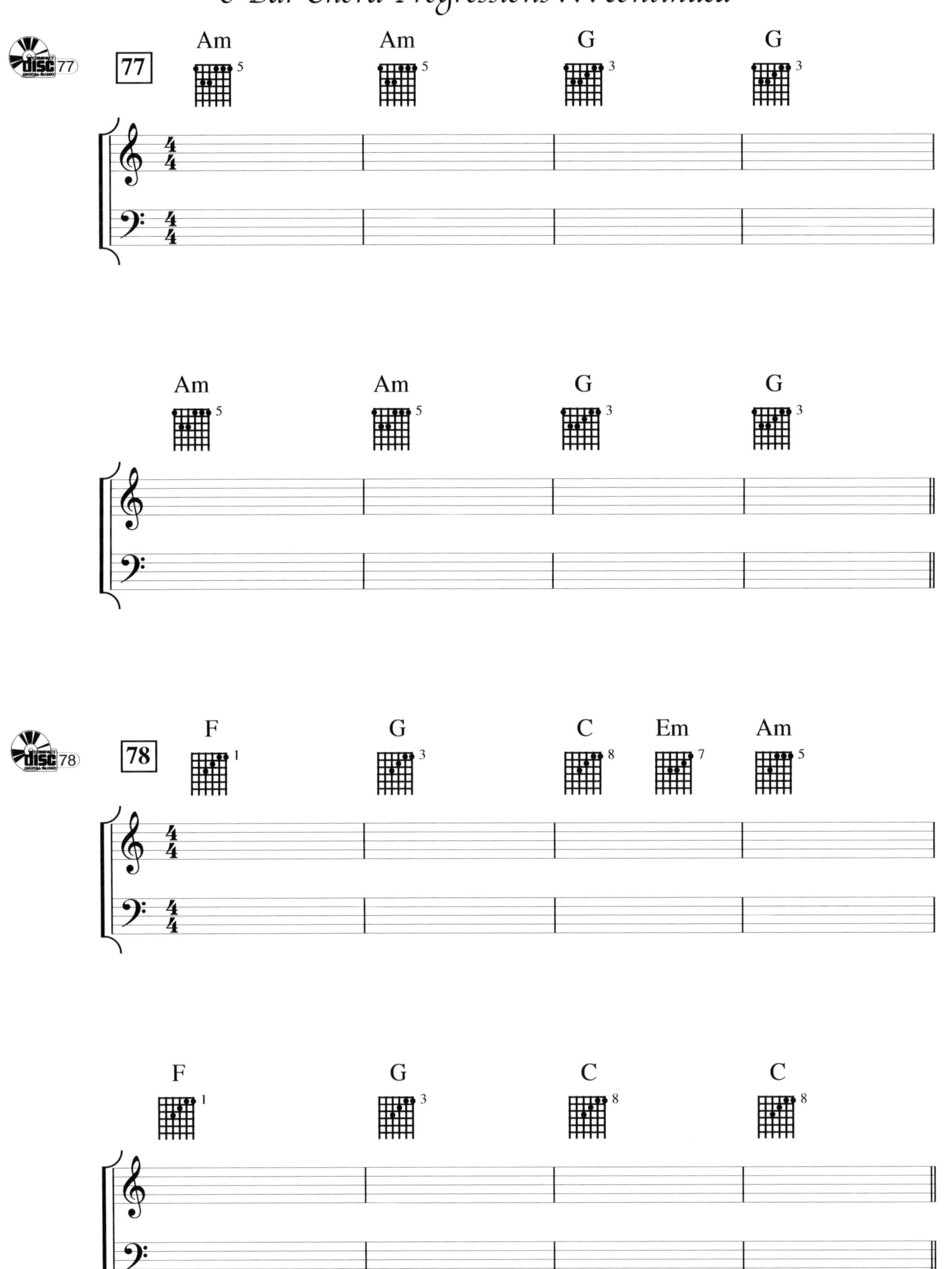

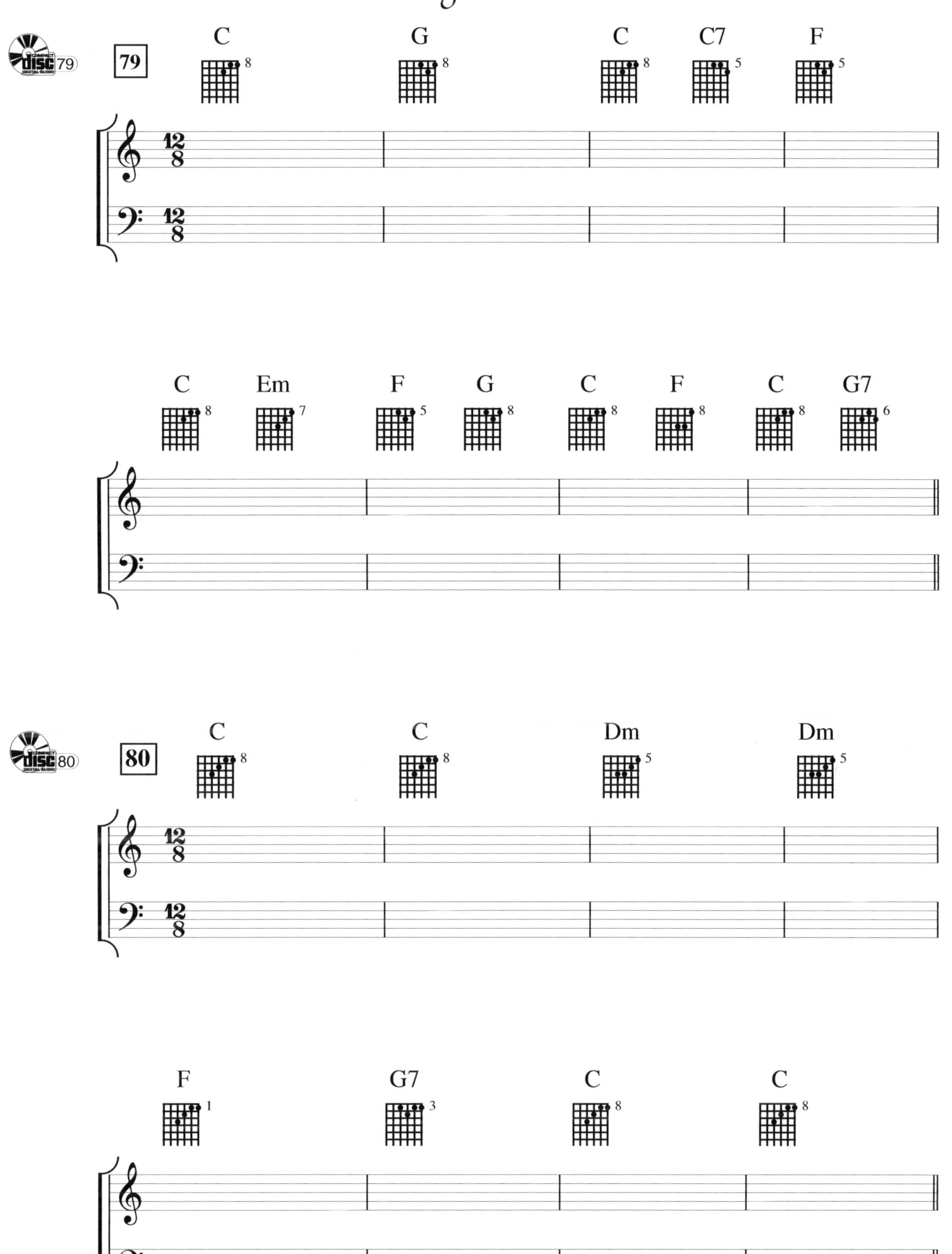
79
79
C
8
G
8
C
8
C7
5
F
5
12
8
12
8
C
8
Em
7
F
5
G
8
C
8
F
8
C
8
G7
6
80
80
C
8
C
8
Dm
5
Dm
5
12
8
12
8
F
1
G7
3
C
8
C
8

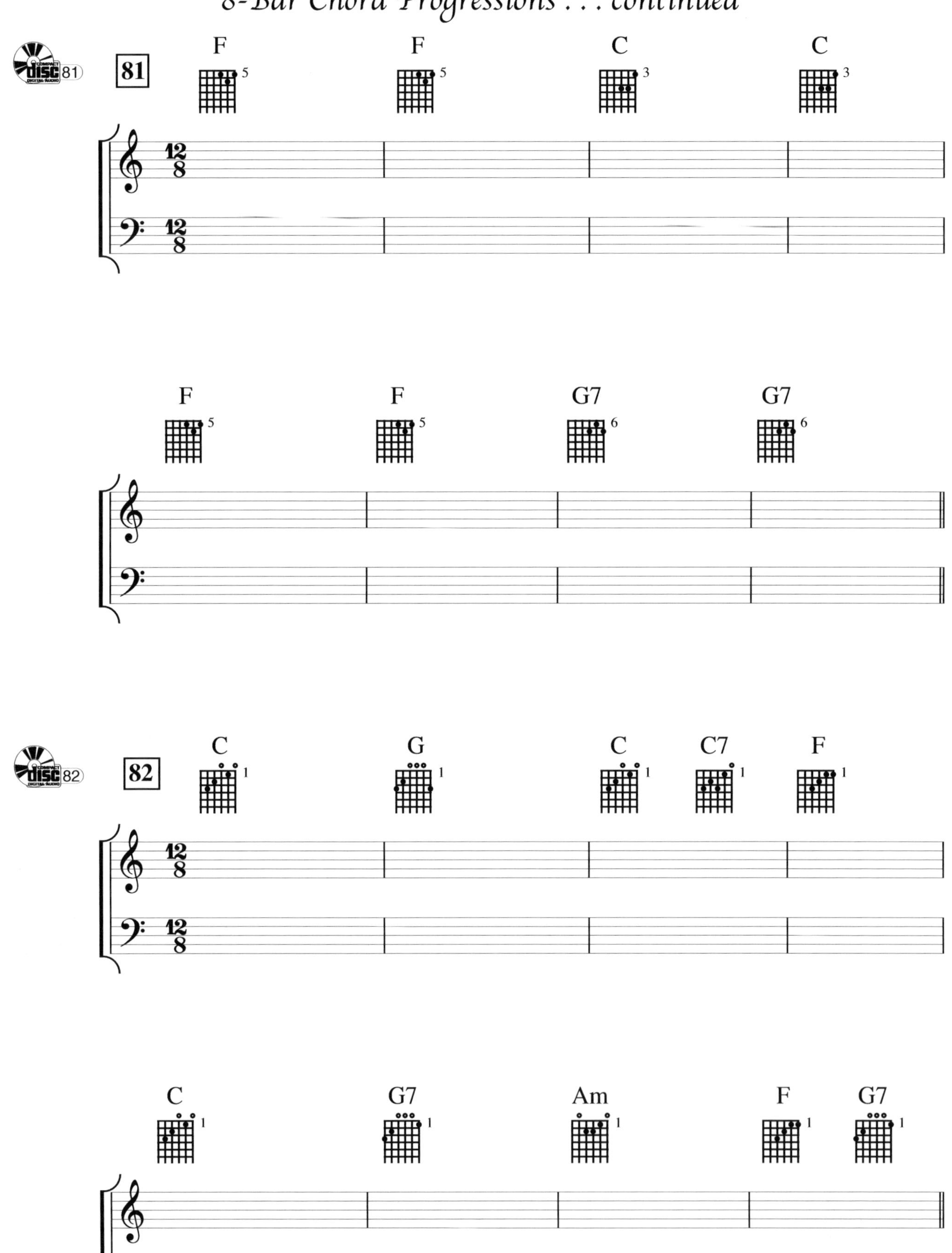
81
81
F
5
F
5
C
3
C
3
F
5
F
5
G7
6
G7
6
82
82
C
1
G
1
C
1
C7
1
F
1
C
1
G7
1
Am
1
F
1
G7
1

8-Bar Chord Progressions . . . continued

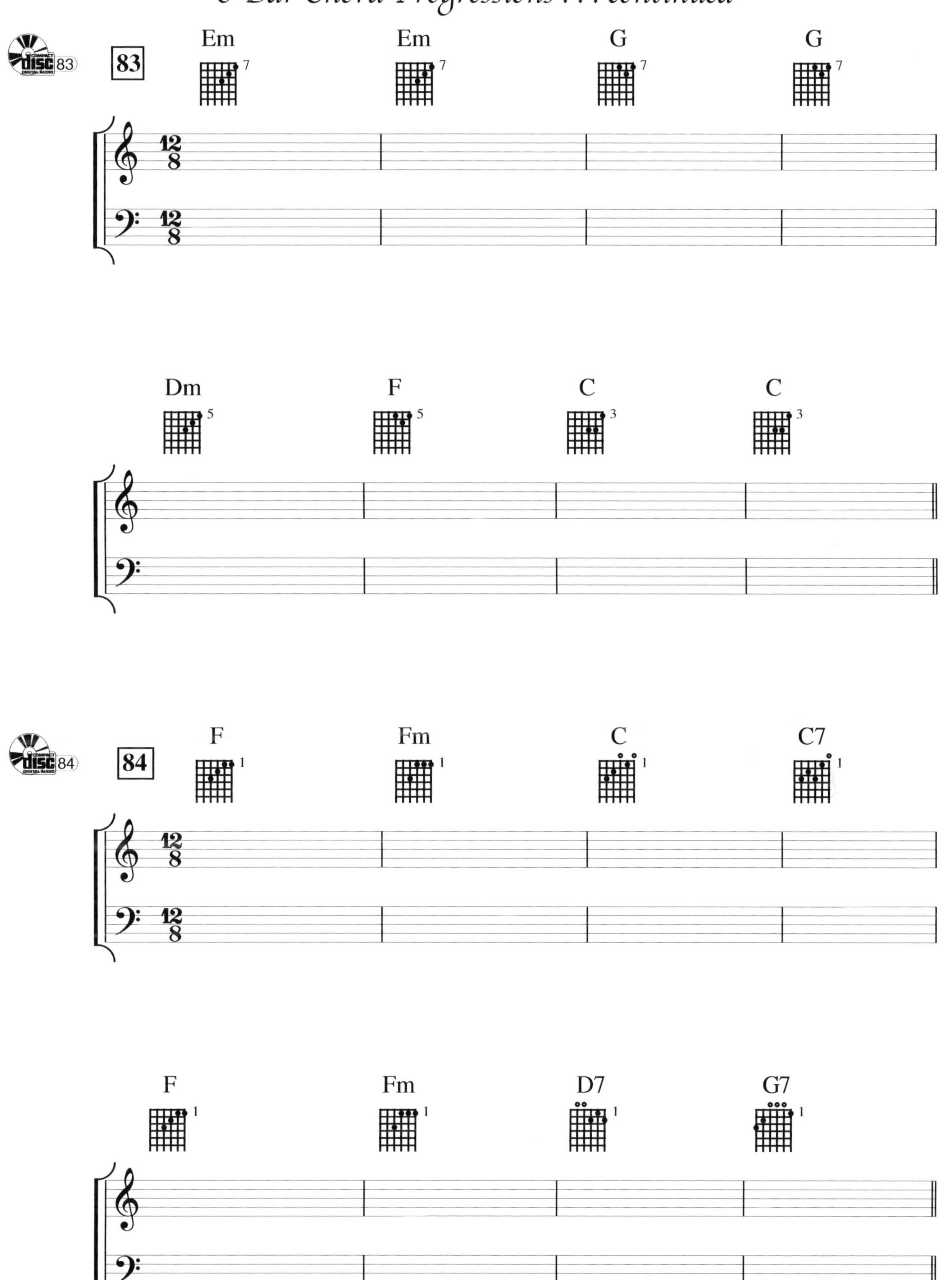

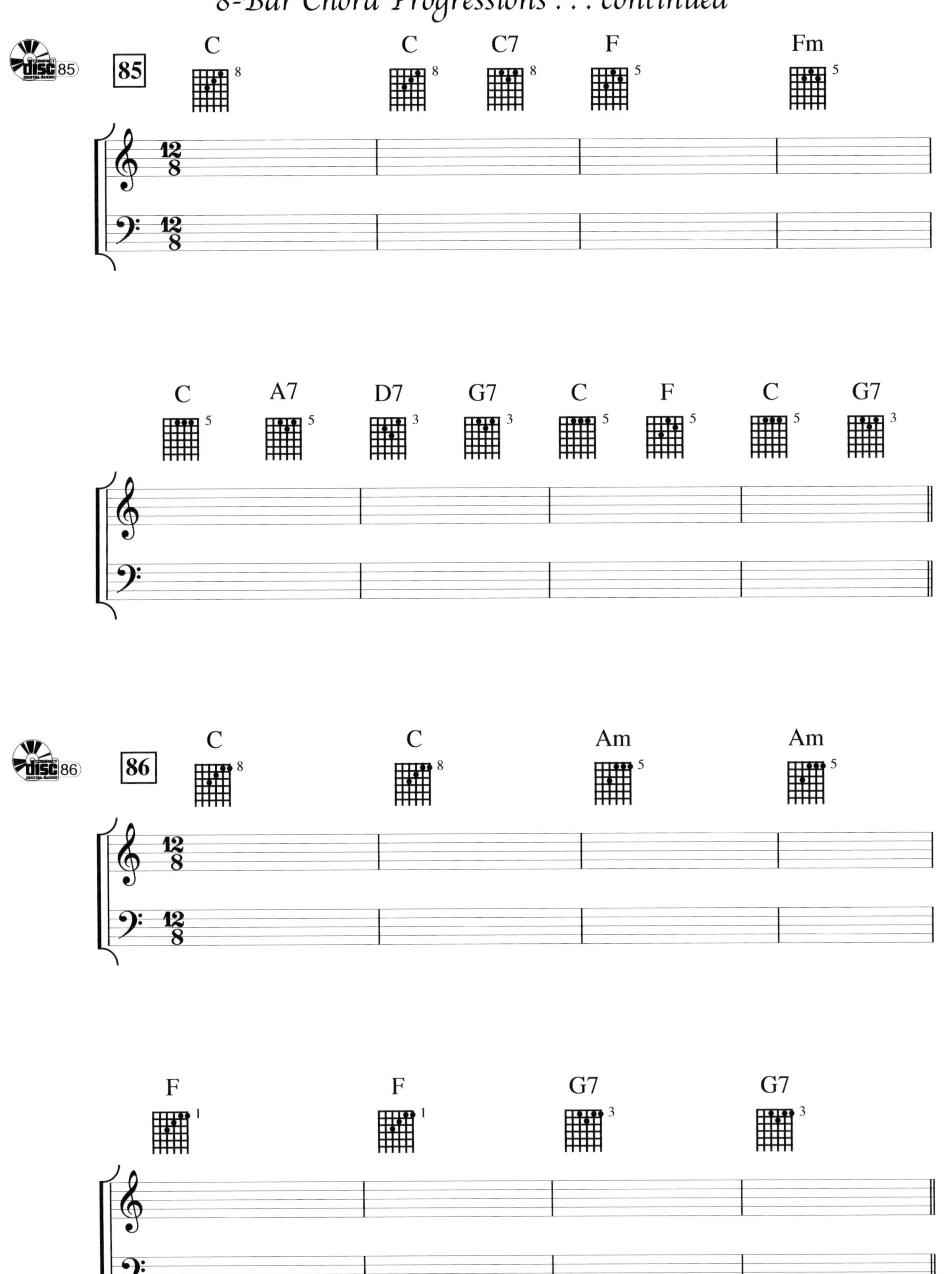
85
85
C
8
C
8
C7
8
F
5
Fm
5
12
8
12
8
C
5
A7
5
D7
3
G7
3
C
5
F
5
C
5
G7
3
86
86
C
8
C
8
Am
5
Am
5
12
8
12
8
F
1
F
1
G7
3
G7
3

4-Bar Minor-Key Chord Progressions

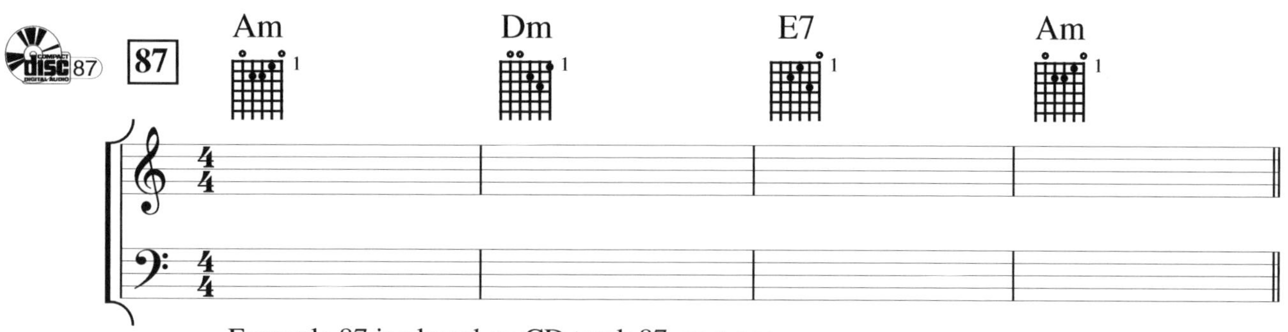

Example 87 is played on CD track 87, part one.

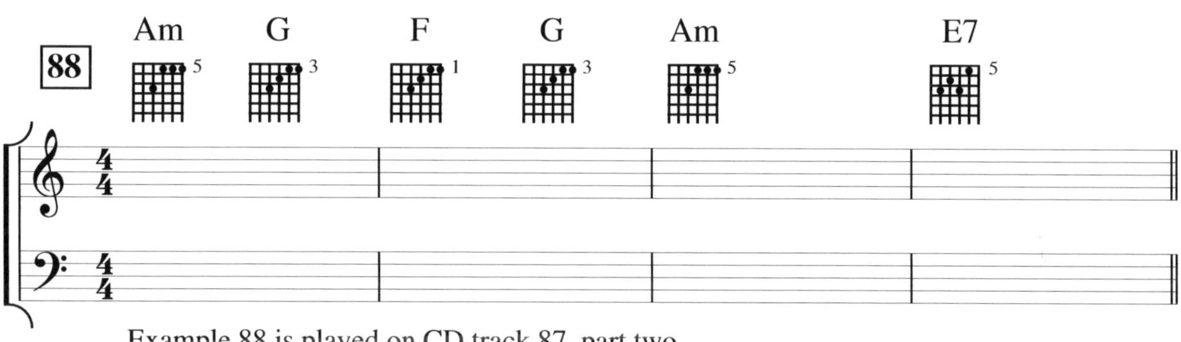

Example 88 is played on CD track 87, part two.

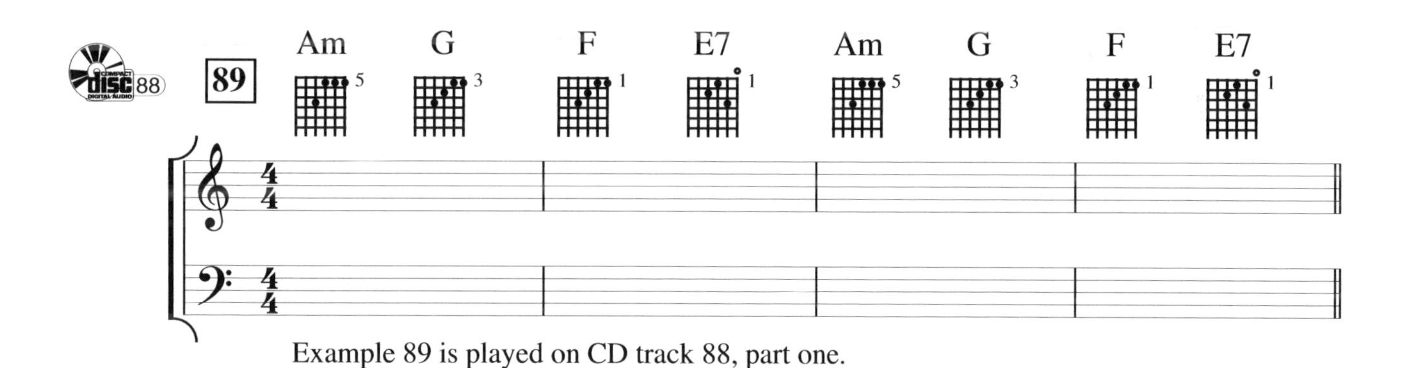

Example 89 is played on CD track 88, part one.

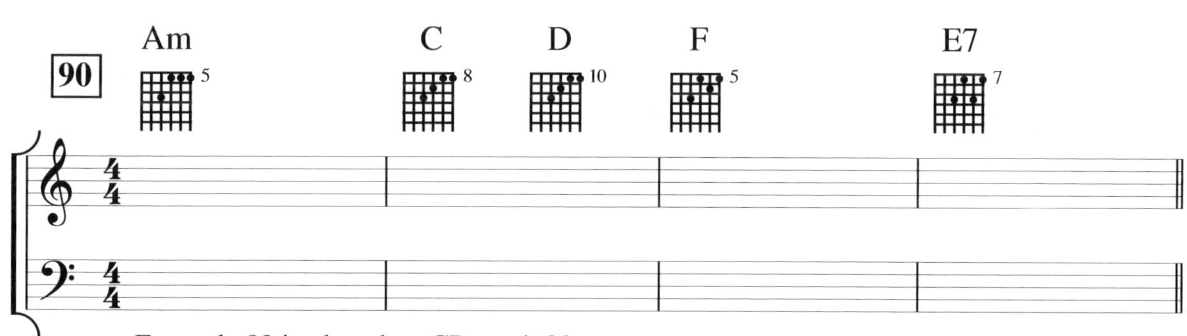

Example 89 is played on CD track 88, part two.

8-Bar Minor-Key Chord Progressions

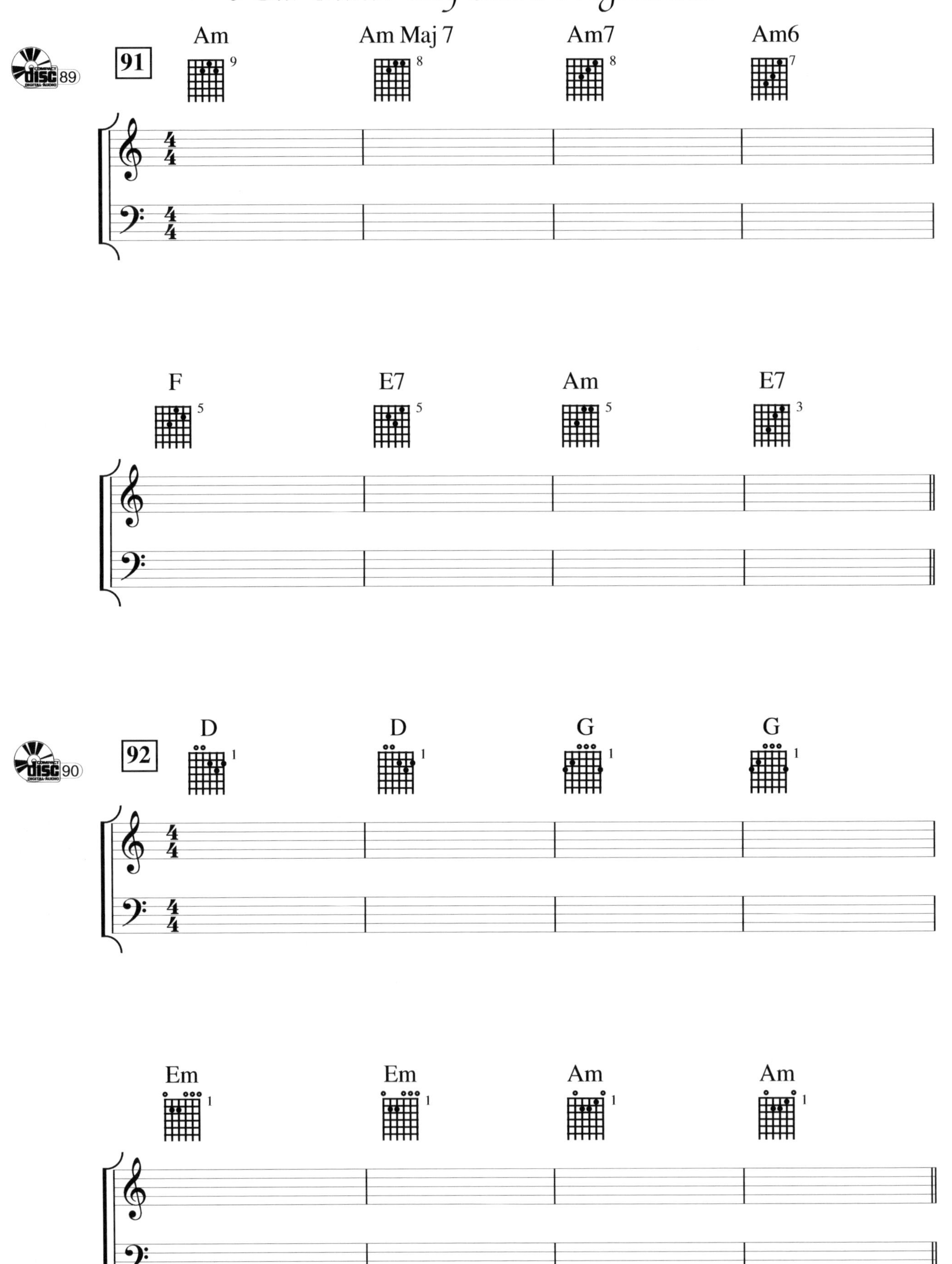

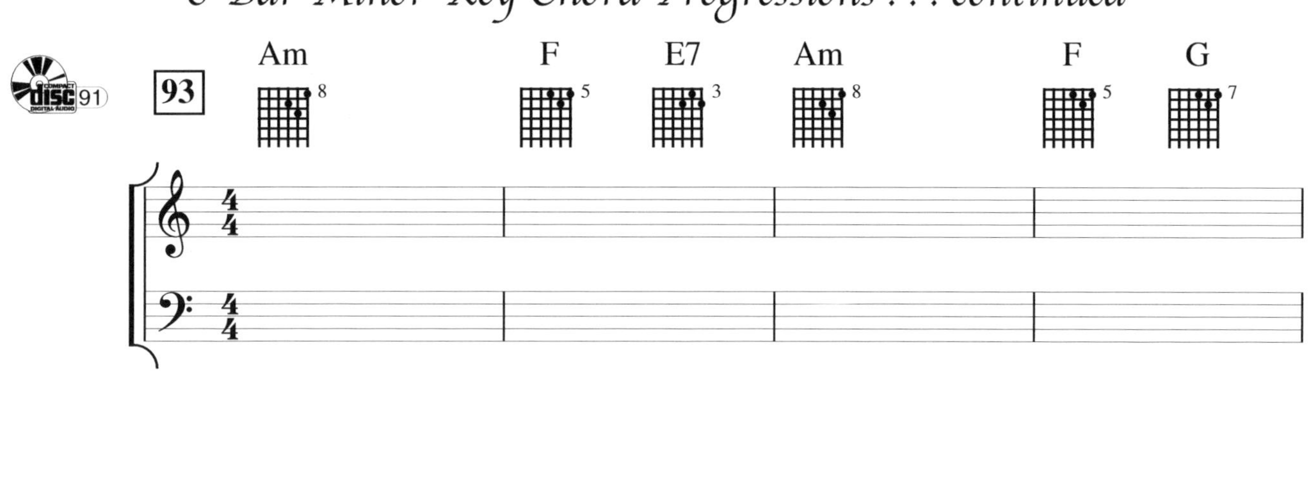
91
93
Am
8
F
5
E7
3
Am
8
F
5
G
7

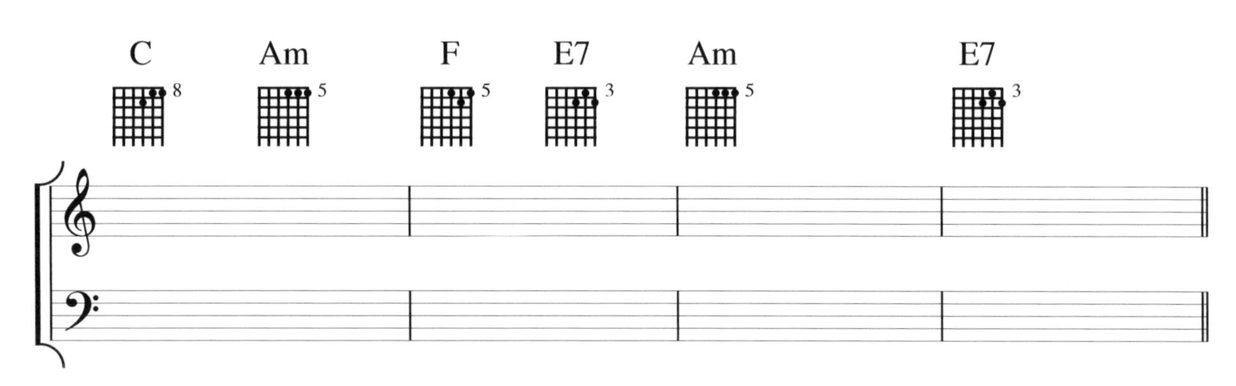
C
8
Am
5
F
5
E7
3
Am
5
E7
3

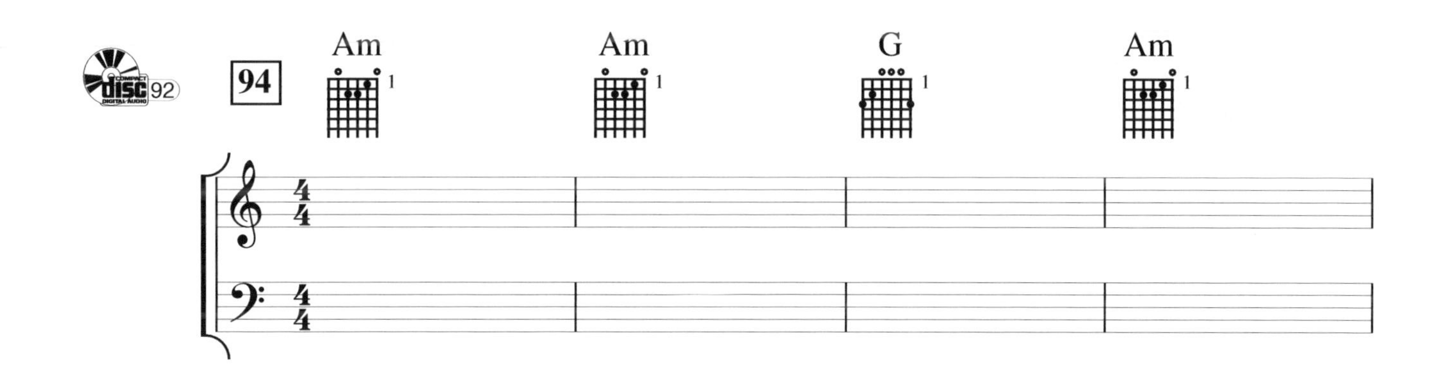
92
94
Am
1
Am
1
G
1
Am
1

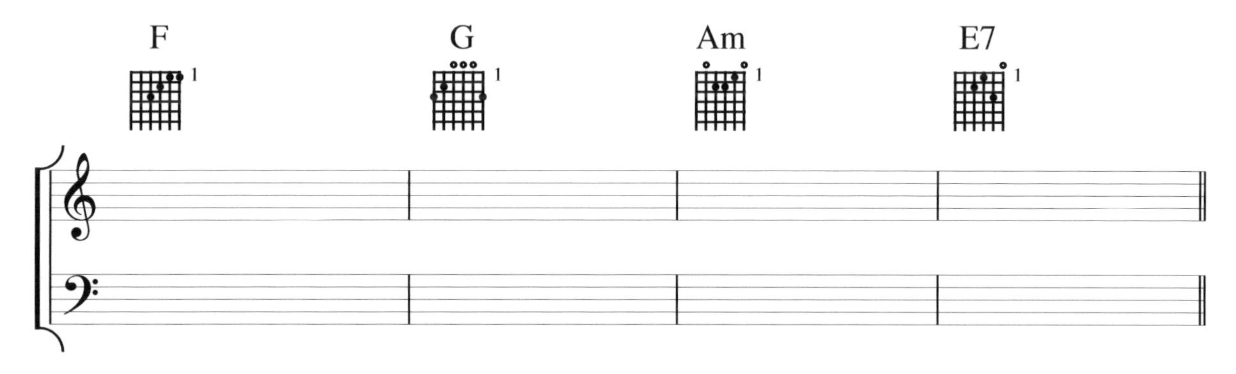
F
1
G
1
Am
1
E7
1

8-Bar Blues Progressions

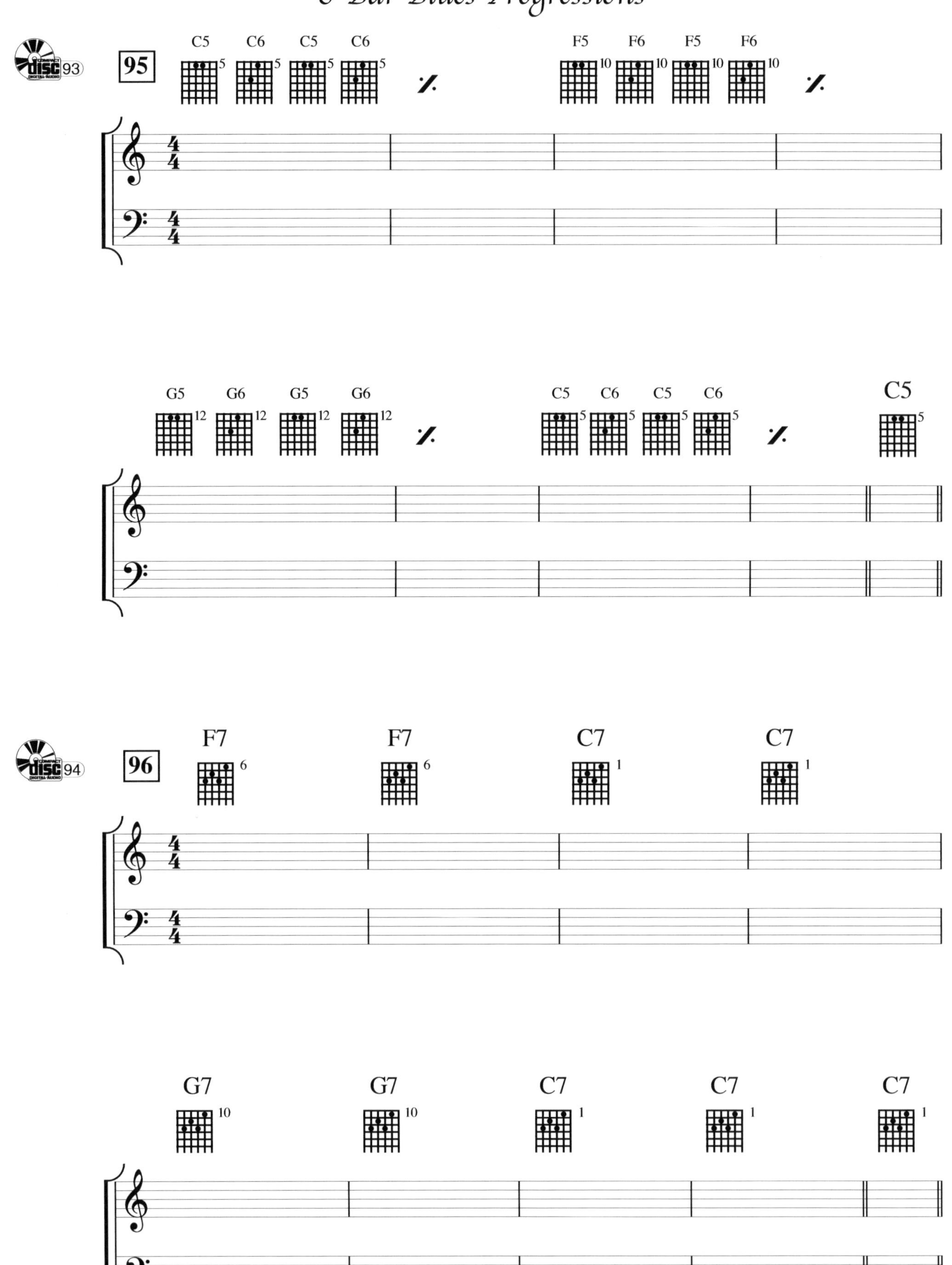

8-Bar Blues Progressions . . . continued

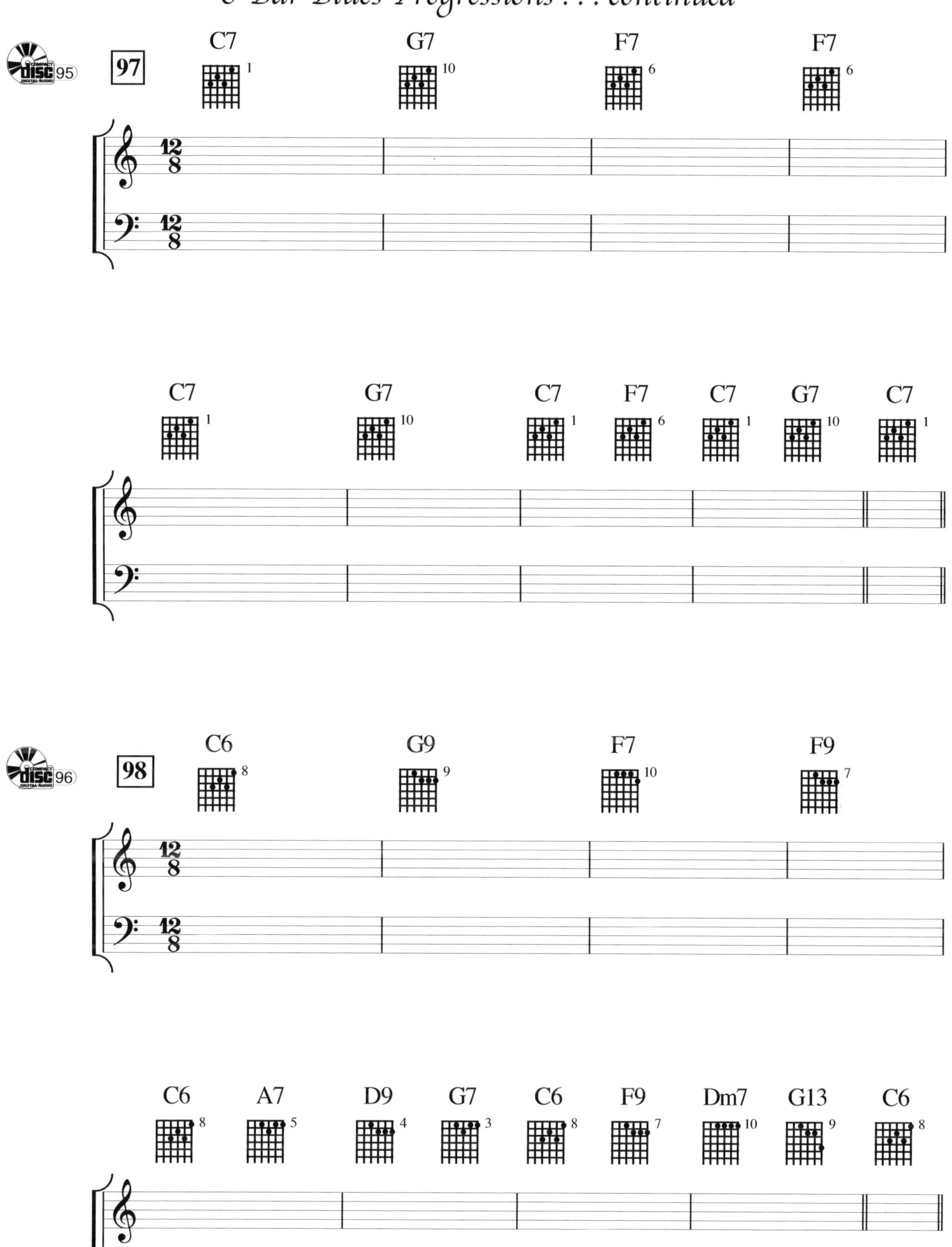

12-Bar Blues Progressions

Learn more blues progressions with the following Mel Bay book/CD by Larry McCabe:

- **101 Essential Blues Progressions**

12-Bar Blues Progressions

Solo like a blues guitar wizard with the following Mel Bay book/CD by Larry McCabe:
• **101 Red Hot Jazz Blues Guitar Licks and Solos**

12-Bar Blues Progressions

Blues in C minor

Famous Rock Rhythms

Each of the rhythms shown below has been used in hundreds of popular rock songs. Other than the "backbeat" rhythm–and, perhaps, the "Twist"–there is no official name for any of these patterns. For many of them, I have supplied the name of a classic rock song that uses that particular rhythm (song titles are surrounded by quote marks). You can make up your own name for each example if you wish.

Each rhythm can be played in many ways by varying accents, chords, and tempo.

The Backbeat Rhythm

The flagship rhythm of rock and roll contains accents on the second and fourth beats.

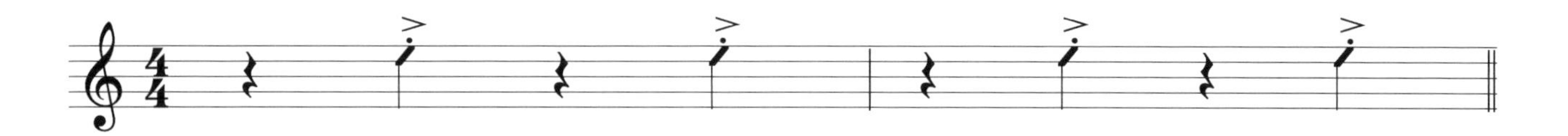

The Eighth Note Rhythm

This produces a driving effect in straight time. It can also be played as a R&B shuffle in 12/8 time. It's easy to vary this rhythm by using different patterns of accents (see the "Twist," below).

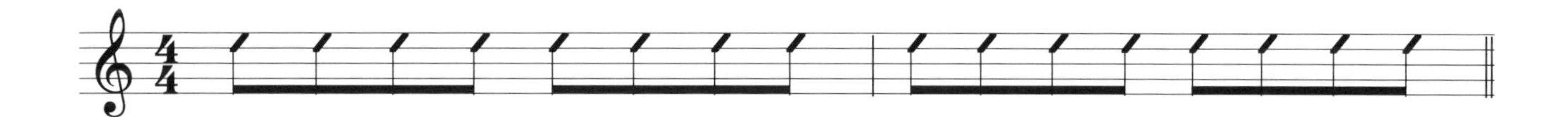

The "Twist" Rhythm

The rhythmic effect is created by accenting the second beat, the fourth beat, and the upbeat of four. Notice that the accents are applied to a plain old Eighth Note Rhythm (see above). Hail, Hail, Chubby Checker!

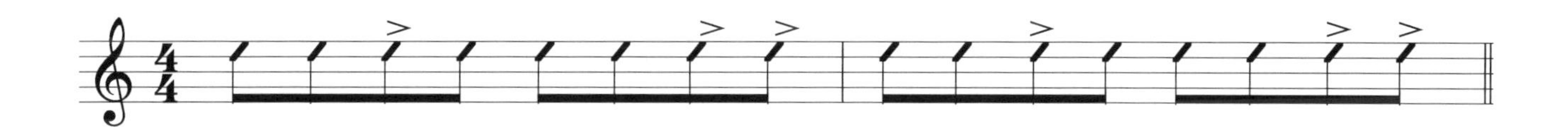

The 5-6 Rhythm

This rhythm involves a "rocking" back and forth between the fifth and sixth tones of a major chord. The rhythm harmonizes with major triads as well as dominant seventh chords.

When played in straight time, the 5-6 rhythm sounds like Chuck Berry. Played as a slow shuffle, it produces a traditional blues sound.

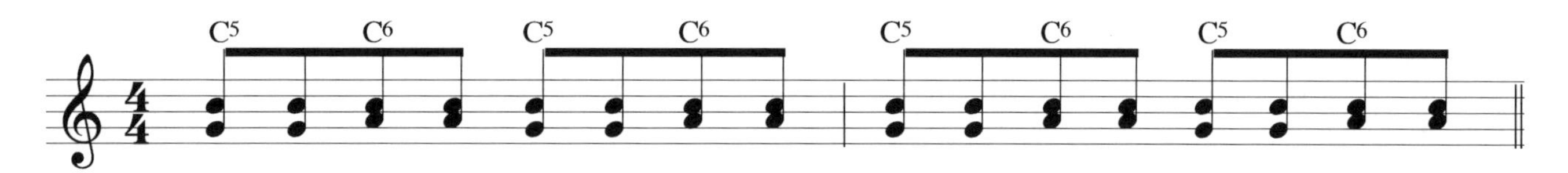

The "Rock Around the Clock" Rhythm

An exciting, honking rhythm that dates back to the great 40's jump blues of Louis Jordan.

The 50's Triplet Rhythm

This rhythm is usually played slowly, using arpeggios or broken chords. The I-vim-IV-V7 chord progression is a favorite harmonic setting for this style. Play this and presto–instant fifties!

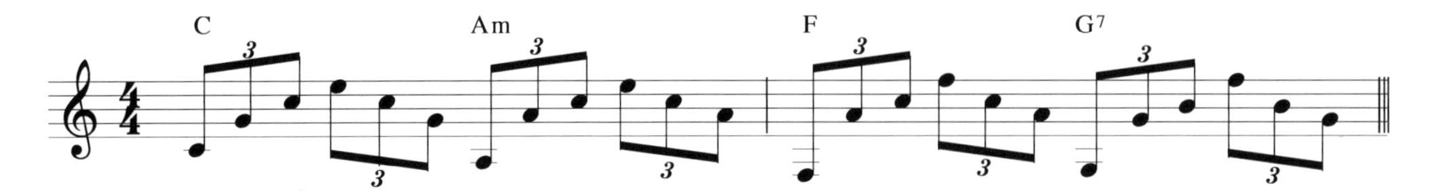

The Power Chord Rhythm

The term "power chord" is a somewhat pompous title for a simple interval of a tonic tone and its fifth. Harmonically ambiguous, this interval can represent any of the following chord types:
1) Major; 2) Minor; 3) Dominant seventh.

To guitar players: Always play "power chords" on the middle to lower strings of the guitar. Distortion is commonly added. All notes should be played with a down-pick strum. Experiment with accents and rests.

The Bo Diddley Rhythm

The Bo Diddley rhythm adds a new twist to the traditional calypso rhythm. Far from serene, this rhythm is perfect for inciting rowdy, uninhibited dancing and other shameless social exhibitions. The rhythm in the first measure, minus the staccato markings, is a standard Calypso folk rhythm.

The "Not Fade Away" Rhythm

This rhythm combines elements of calypso, Bo Diddley, and Buddy Holly. The amplified result is a solid, fairly heavy beat for dancing.

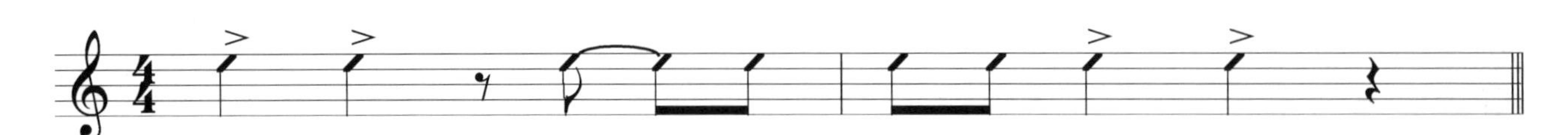

The "Louie, Louie" Rhythm

Have you ever asked yourself, "Why didn't I write this thing?"

Played and loved by every garage band in the world, the pattern is on permanent exhibit at the Rock Strums Hall of Fame.

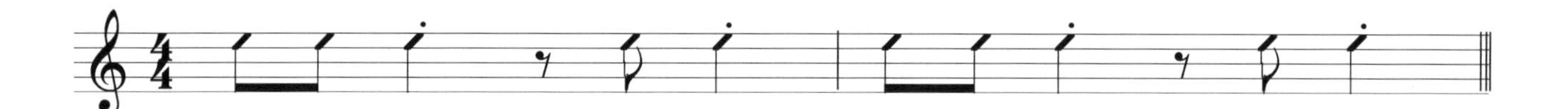

The "Wild Thing" Rhythm

This rhythm, heard in many songs, works equally well in heavy, medium, and light rock songs. It is important that guitar players play the second sixteenth note in each measure with an up pick.

The "Get off My Cloud" Rhythm

Notice the similarity between this rhythm and the previous one. Add three chords and you're in hitsville!

The "Sunshine of Your Love" Rhythm

Although not as common as some of the other rhythms in this section, I have included this one to demonstrate the effective use of space. Sparse patterns like this one are sometimes played in rhythmic unison on the guitar (or keyboard) and the bass.

The Basic <u>Latin</u> Rhythm

Latin rhythms are used in all rock styles from classic to "saltwater" to heavy rock. A Latin rhythm is syncopated–accented notes or chords are frequently played on upbeats–and played in straight time.

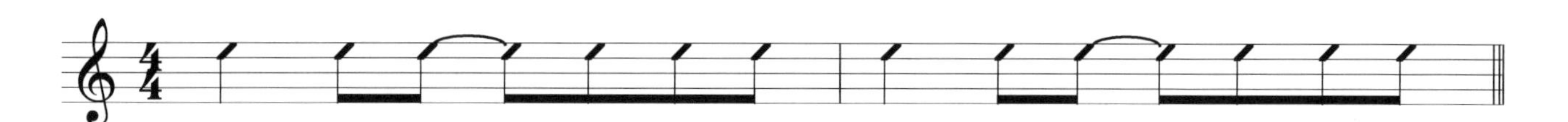

The "Hang on, Sloopy" Rhythm

Here's another way to achieve a light Latin syncopation. It's typical, but not necessary, to change chords on the 4 and strum in the first measure.

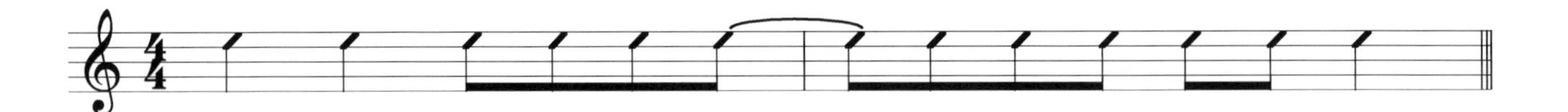

The "La Bamba" Rhythm

Still another twist on the basic Latin rhythm. If you need a good dance rhythm, this one works very well. Try changing chords on the following beats: 1) The upbeat of 4 in the first bar; 2) Beat 3 of measure two.

The "Sloop John B." Rhythm

Now for a classic Caribbean strum for those "saltwater" gigs. Played at a moderate to peppy tempo, this rhythm has a chugging, bubbly sound. For happy songs, happy people, and happy times.

The Boom Chick-a Boom Rhythm

This triplet rhythm is ideal for classic R&B or 50's music. The strum works best when played at a moderate tempo. Try playing two beats each of C, Am, F, and G7 to this rhythm for a classic 50's sound.

The "Smokestack Lightning" Rhythm

Here we have the rawboned sound of the Mississippi Delta. The riff is always played as a slow blues shuffle. Guitar players like to play this against either an E7 or Em chord.

How To Transpose Chord Progressions

The chord progressions in this book are written in either C major or A minor. However, you should also learn to play the progressions in other keys. The following table shows the scale tones in seven popular major keys. Refer to the table when transposing a chord progression to or from any of these keys.

KEY	SCALE TONES							
	1	2	3	4	5	6	7	8
C	C	D	E	F	G	A	B	C
G	G	A	B	C	D	E	F♯	G
D	D	E	F♯	G	A	B	C♯	D
A	A	B	C♯	D	E	F♯	G♯	A
E	E	F♯	G♯	A	B	C♯	D♯	E
F	F	G	A	B♭	C	D	E	F
B♭	B♭	C	D	E♭	F	G	A	B♭

USING THE TABLE TO TRANSPOSE A SIMPLE CHORD PROGRESSION

1. We will use the following KEY OF C chord progression as our example:

I C / / / I C / / / I F / / / I F / / / I

Transposing begins with assigning a number to each chord in the progression. Because the C chord is built on the first tone of the C scale, it will be called the I chord (Roman numerals are used to identify chords). The F note, being built on the fourth tone of the C scale, will be called IV. Our chord progression has now been translated into numbers that can be applied to any key:

I I / / / I I / / / I IV / / / I IV / / / I

2. We will now transpose this progression to the key of G using the following procedure:

a) To find the I chord in G, name the first tone in the G scale. Result: G = I in the key of G.

b) To find the IV chord in G, name the fourth tone in the G scale. Result: C = IV in the key of G.

Our new chords are G (I), and C (IV). The chord progression looks like this in G major:

I I IV IV
I G / / / I G / / / I C / / / I C / / / I

Once you learn the position of every tone in each scale, it becomes a snap to transpose chords.

COMPARISON OF THE BASIC CHORDS IN THE KEYS OF C AND G

	I	iim	iiim	IV	V7	vim	viidim
Key of C	C	Dm	Em	F	G7	Am	Bdim
Key of G	G	Am	Bm	C	D7	Em	F#dim

A complete discussion of chord theory is beyond the scope of this book. However, the table of basic chords (above) is included to show you that some Roman numerals carry additional information such as m, 7, dim, and so on. For example, Dm is *iim* in the key of C, not just "2." Notice also that minor chords are labeled with lowercase Roman numerals (Ex: iim instead of IIM). Another example: The G7 chord is V7 in the key of C, not just "5." The V chord in C is G; V7 in the same key is G7.

Mel Bay Book/CD sets by Larry McCabe

SONG WRITING / THEORY / ALL INSTRUMENTS

- You Can Teach Yourself® Song Writing (94823BCD)
- 101 Essential Country Chord Progressions (99043BCD)
- Music Theory 101 (99393)

BLUES GUITAR

- 101 Blues Guitar Turnaround Licks (95360BCD)
- 101 Mississippi Delta Blues Fingerpicking Licks (96241BCD)
- 101 Bad-to-the-Bone Blues Guitar Rhythm Patterns (97760BCD)
- 101 Dynamite Slide Guitar Licks in Open E Tuning* (97223BCD)
- Famous Blues Guitar Lines (98428BCD)

ROCK GUITAR

- Famous Rock Guitar Lines (98430BCD)

FINGERSTYLE GUITAR

- 101 Mississippi Delta Blues Fingerpicking Licks (96241BCD)

COUNTRY GUITAR

- 101 Nashville Style Guitar Licks (95447BCD)
- Famous Country Guitar Lines (98427BCD)

SLIDE GUITAR

- 101 Dynamite Slide Guitar Licks in Open E Tuning* (97223BCD)

SWING/JAZZ GUITAR

- 101 Red-Hot Swing Guitar Licks (97335BCD)

BLUEGRASS GUITAR/MANDOLIN

- 101 Red Hot Bluegrass Guitar Licks and Solos (99445BCD)
- 101 Red Hot Bluegrass Mandolin Licks and Solos (99446BCD)

GUITAR/BANJO/AND UKE

- 101 Three-Chord Songs for Guitar, Banjo, and Uke (99476)

BLUES BASS

- 101 Blues Patterns for Bass Guitar (95330BCD)
- Famous Blues Bass Lines (98429BCD)

JAZZ BASS

- 101 Amazing Jazz Bass Patterns (97336BCD)

***Text in English and Spanish**

38903382R00029

Made in the USA
San Bernardino, CA
14 September 2016